Pleasure Erased

Pleasure Erased
The Clitoris Unthought

Catherine Malabou

Translated by Carolyn Shread

polity

Originally published in French as *Le plaisir effacé: clitoris et pensée*
© 2020, Éditions Payot & Rivages

This English translation © 2022, Polity Press

This work received the French Voices Award for excellence in publication and translation.
French Voices is a program created and funded by the French Embassy in the United States
and FACE Foundation (French American Cultural Exchange).
French Voices logo designed by Serge Bloch.

Polity Press
65 Bridge Street
Cambridge CB2 1UR, UK

Polity Press
111 River Street
Hoboken, NJ 07030, USA

ISBN-13: 978-1-5095-4992-4 hardback
ISBN-13: 978-1-5095-4993-1 paperback

A catalogue record for this book is available from the British Library.

Library of Congress Control Number: 2022930397

Typeset in 12.5 on 15 pt Adobe Garamond
by Cheshire Typesetting Ltd, Cuddington, Cheshire
Printed and bound in Great Britain by CPI Group (UK) Ltd, Croydon

The publisher has used its best endeavors to ensure that the URLs for external websites
referred to in this book are correct and active at the time of going to press. However, the
publisher has no responsibility for the websites and can make no guarantee that a site will
remain live or that the content is or will remain appropriate.

Every effort has been made to trace all copyright holders, but if any have been overlooked the
publisher will be pleased to include any necessary credits in any subsequent reprint or edition.

For further information on Polity, visit our website:
politybooks.com

*In memory of Anne Dufourmantelle,
echoing her meditation on gentleness*

Clitoris, mysterious ruby, swaying, jewel-like shimmer on the chest of a deity.

(Pierre Louÿs, *Poesies érotiques : La femme; La trophée des vulves légendaires; Pybrac*, Paris: Editinter, 2010)

Contents

Translator's Preface

Translating the Emergence of the *Point Médian*, or Clitoridian Anarchy in the Text

In Lori Chamberlain's "Gender and Metaphorics of Translation" (1988), she drew attention to the many phallocentric ways in which translation was conceptualized, citing George Steiner's references to penetration as just one of too many paradigms of domination. Given my past theorizing as I translate Catherine Malabou, it would be no surprise if I were to propose here that we consider translation from a clitoral perspective. I could describe how the translator combs though the text, stroking it over and over in an act of love and care to find its *gioia* in a new language. It's an obvious metaphor, another to add to our collection, since these tropes are of the trade. But might I find more than another analogy? What does this most recent Malabou offer for thinking translating and its pleasures, inked or erased?

In this translation, it was a moment of hesitation that opened new plasticities: what to do with the *point médian*? The *point médian* is one of several new linguistic phenomena emerging as French grapples with its grammatical sexism. Reworking a male bias deep in the structures of the language, some French speakers have sought to resolve the dilemma, shared with other Romance languages, by which linguistic norms produce a hypervisibility of gender along with a privileging of the masculine. This is all the more imperative because French schoolchildren are taught, over and again, *le masculin l'emporte sur le féminin* – that is, "the masculine prevails over the feminine" – since, in verb conjugations and agreements, the masculine is always the default: girls learn that, even if there are 100 of them and 1 boy joins the group, the adjective must be changed from the feminine to the masculine form. One solution has been the *point médian,* or mid·dot punctuation mark, as, for instance, in the greeting "*Cher·e·s ami·e·s*" in which masculine (*ami*) and feminine (*amie*) forms of "friend" are combined. The mid·dot gesture is an improvement on

the previous use of parentheses "ami(e)s," imply-
ing as it does a lesser importance to the enclosed
feminine. This embedded sexism is experienced
as problematic on multiple fronts, not least of
which is the necessity to specify a binary male/
female gender. While English is adopting the
"they" pronoun, French equivalents such as the
neologism *iel*, which appears just twice in this
book, are having more difficulty establishing
themselves. The decision of the renowned *Petit
Robert* dictionary to add *iel* to its online edition
in November 2021 is indicative of an early insti-
tutionalization of the term, even as it provoked
furious debate. Another French strategy is to
search out gender neutral language through those
rare nouns that can be used with either gender,
as in "Chers destinataires," or "dear addressees."
Either way, these contortions – including the not
insignificant keyboard challenge presented by
finding the mid·dot that consequently often slips
down to become a period – indicate a need to
shape language, and our language technologies, to
better hold all of our experiences.

The brand-new translator's dilemma is
whether to signal this effort by French to be
more inclusive, or else to use gender neutral

terms readily available in English. In this translation, to acknowledge the way the French reforms itself through the plastic explosive of the mid·dot, I often alert the reader with the phrase "be they he or she," a concatenation of pronouns that echoes debates in English while avoiding the implied essentialist binary in "man or woman." I thus opted to retain and highlight the presence of these moments of revolt rather than using the suppleness of English to hide that awkward move reminiscent of the "he/she" that I have since replaced with "they" in other recent translations. After all, if I erase the visual shock of the controversial mid·dot, I lose the challenge to the normativity of French as determined by authorities such as the Académie française, which is firmly against such innovations: in 2021, it declared that *l'écriture inclusive* is an aberration – such a mortal threat to the French language, indeed, that it was banned in schools. This may be the view of the *Immortels*, as members of the Académie are known, but language is notoriously plastic, shaping and shaped by our realities, and here it is, the mid·dot, already present on 15 occasions in this latest Malabou. I read these moments as textual clitorises, a tentative touching in spite of censure. Is it the influence of the Anglophone environment in which her thought circulates and engages – perhaps even a translational effect? No doubt partly, but Malabou is also shaking up French on her own account – after all, as she states, unforgettably, here: "The clitoris is an anarchist" (p. 119). So, it may well be that the venerable institution of the Académie française, founded in 1634 to protect, foster and celebrate the French language, with its 737 members over the centuries – yes, 10 of them women – is, so to speak, missing the point.

Turning to the anarchist clitoris, the punctuated pleasure represented by the mid·dot is symbolic of the stakes at play in this book, Malabou's most recent reflection on plasticity. Here, she works through the systematic unthinking of the clitoris in philosophy. In so doing, she develops the structuring concept of *l'écart* in concert with the clitoris. It is important to distinguish her conception, translated here as "caesura," from the use of the same word by Jacques Rancière, in whose work it is translated alternately as "interval" or "gap," as well as from Jacques Derrida's *différance*. Malabou is bringing new forms to light, forms that relate time, space, politics and power in their own distinctive manner. We look forward to her next book on anarchy to further develop the role of the clitoris as a plastic opportunity that might – indeed, must – herald the caesura of our era. Certainly, if we are to respond to the existential threat of climate change, it will be on condition of establishing permaculture in place of clear cutting, a reclaiming of pleasures erased as fields for new modes of thought.

Malabou directs us toward the newly emergent forms that artists such as Sophia Wallace are bringing to popular consciousness. Revealing the beauteous form of the clitoris, thanks to the research of Australian urologist Dr. Helen O'Connell in 1998, Wallace's first anatomically correct sculpture of the clitoris, *Ἀδάμας* or *Unconquerable* (2013), takes down the invisibility and moves us toward a new understanding of clitoral bodies and pleasures, disarming the status quo as she does so since "democracy without cliteracy is phallusy" (www.sophiawallace. art). Or, to deploy the potent term imported by translators of the 1970s Italian radical feminist Carla Lonzi, whose thought Malabou productively engages here, this aesthetic reformulation is a "clitoridian" act.

The affirmation of the neologism "clitoridian" as a self-consciously politicized alternative to the standard medical "clitoral" is an important contribution to this new body of thought, signaling its distinctiveness. While *clitoridea* exists in Italian, just as *clitoridien·ne* exists in French, the English clips the end of the word to the short "clitoral." Other English translations – for instance, of the work of Luce Irigaray by Carolyn Burke and Gillian C. Gill – respect the English term; here, I seek to reinforce "clitoridian" as a second available term that offers us a productive and generative neologism. Our translations both track and advance our histories and epistemologies: here, we look to a clitoridian future.

Feminist translation studies could well use the distinction between a clitoral and a clitoridian translation theory, with "clitoral" revealing the other side of a binary and "clitoridian" establishing a realm of sexual difference along with the political determination to find another relation to power, one that is "not a power relation" (p. 119). These two alternate approaches might be helpful as feminist translation evolves and builds momentum, from its emergence as a creative practice in Canada from the 1970s, and theorization from there globally from the mid-1990s onwards. Just as translators have worked alongside changing feminisms, so too they have plasticized the ways we think about translating strategies, goals and effects. In the moment of radical digital communication revolution we are living, as artificial intelligence increasingly takes hold of our linguistic and translational practices, now is the time for a return to our plastic bodies and brains to foment clitoridian anarchy in translation.

Carolyn Shread

Foreword

by Alexandra Kleeman

Life in the twenty-first century unfolds beneath a ceaseless, anxiety-ridden gaze that is fixated on the body: how should it be fed, how should you optimize its sleeping and waking, how can you burn the fat from it, how can you sculpt it into the shape of a beach body or an hourglass? As a pandemic swept the world, this fixation on restoring visibility to the physiological has moved inward, to the nasal passageways and lungs and immune system, to the surveillance of its interior spaces and contemplation of its openness to infection. Several decades devoted to the body's reincorporation within scholarly thought and practice have brought corporeality back from the periphery, both as a holistic unit and as a collection of important parts. But, curiously, a crucial part has been left out of these analyses: the clitoris, the existence of which is glimpsed in elision, as though something dangerous would happen if one were to linger too long upon it.

Catherine Malabou devotes this volume to locating and relocating the clitoris in the various discourses – sociopolitical, physiological, philosophical, psychoanalytic – in which it has appeared, touching upon these furtive or dismissive instances and putting them into contact with feminist thinkers such as Irigaray, Lonzi and de Beauvoir who articulated a vital role for the clitoris within thought, subjectivity and society. Malabou writes:

> Still, today, the clitoris bears the trace of a wound against which words wash up like waves, pulling away as soon as they emerge. This is not to say that it is the place of a lack, of the signifier, the letter or object a, b, c or z. It's far more complicated than that, and also far simpler. Even if it is not necessarily a woman's clitoris, the clitoris remains the mysterious place of the feminine. Which means it still hasn't found its place. (p. 12)

That place, for Malabou, is close to the center of philosophy: a point of responsivity, sensitivity and, perhaps most importantly, *pleasure*, which has the potential to organize thinking and living in a liberatory release of the feminine with implications both for women and for those who do not identify as such.

The phallus casts a long shadow. Even after much re-contextualization, the vagina of the popular imagination is defined in terms of lack, rather than the satisfaction and relief of presence. The reintroduction of the clitoris makes these anatomical structures more complicated to read, unsettles the legibility of the schemas handed down by phallogocentric thinking. Malabou reads the clitoris as an interloper in the binary juxtaposition of activity/passivity and pleasure/reproduction, urging on the creation of more densely relational interpretations. Among the assemblage of the vagina are different elements that "harbor no power relation" (p. 67) – elements that, as the author points out in reading Irigaray, harbor no rivalry and exert no pressure. In difference, multiplicity and relation, there lies a counterpoint to the dominant singular.

In other hands, foregrounding an anatomical structure could be regressive, exclusionary.

But, as Malabou leads us through the version of the clitoris that she calls into being, it is clear that the clitoris is a seat of the feminine released from the falsely fixed paradigm of the woman. Furthermore, a clitoridian subject would not be one who replaces the phallus at the center of much thought with a new organ, but would imply a new subject coming into being through the formation of new connections between the intellect and libido. Malabou wishes even to rethink the "essentialism" of essence, writing that "for the Greeks an essence (*eidos*) is movement, the dynamic of coming into presence or appearing. An essence, then, is anything but a nature or fixed instance. The fact that, through a subsequent metaphysical contraction, essence has become just that does not alter its originary plasticity" (p. 70). As in her previous work, the material of the body, whether it be brain or genital, is possessed by a radical plasticity – plasticity in the most fundamental sense, pointing to a transformative potential capable of completely annihilating preceding forms as it brings the new into being.

Because, in Malabou's own words, "philosophy shapes bodies," the acceptance of the clitoris

back into the fold of philosophy is transformative, a movement toward the embodiment of a
different subjectivity. It is the acceptance of the
transformative ability of the body, its tendency to
continue forming, successively, an identity. And
for the reader, the encounter with this text is
rousing, the way touch awakens feeling, and feeling heightens touch. It is a profound sensitization
of philosophy that one finds within these pages –
sensible, and yet capable of losing its head.

Erasures

The clitoris is that piece of grit lodged deep in the shoe of sexual fantasy. In Greek mythology, young Clitoris, renowned for her slight figure, was said to be small "as a pebble." Hidden through the ages, nameless, devoid of artistic representation, absent from medical treatises, often unknown even to women themselves, for centuries the clitoris was but a *scruple*, in the original sense of the term: that seed irritating every step and tormenting the mind.[1] The uncertain etymology of the word derives from its morphology as both "hill" (*kleitoris*) and "clasp" (*kleidos*). Clitoris. The secret nub that remains, resists, unsettles the conscience and wounds the heel, the only organ whose sole purpose is pleasure – that is, the only one with "no use." None at all, the immense *niente*, the all or nothing of female pleasure.

The word was first used in an anatomical context by Rufus of Ephesus, a Greek physician who lived in the first and second century CE and who played with its synonyms in a tantalizing manner: "The muscular area of flesh in the middle [of the cleft] is the 'young girl' or 'myrtle berry.' Some call it the 'under-skin' and others, the 'clitoris.' And they call 'clitorizing' the lustful touching of this area."[2] Gabriele Falloppio, after whom the Fallopian tubes are named, claimed to discover the clitoris in 1561. The word *cleitoris* appeared in French in 1575 in a work by Ambroise Paré but the term was mysteriously removed from his *Œuvres* in 1585.[3] Hardly on the page, already was the clitoris erased.

Fast-forward to the twenty-first century. A gynecologist is explaining to a dumb-struck male audience how the clitoris responds to a penis, dildo, fingers or tongue during love-making, describing how it moves and the form it takes during penetration or stroking.[4] She describes how the clitoris is the vagina's accomplice, its partner. But also how it plays solo. How the clitoris enjoys a dual erotic orientation: swaying along with the movements of the vagina during penetration, but also stiffening and standing up like a crest. Sometimes both, other times just one. Opting for neither one, the clitoris confounds dichotomies.

This double life, which presents a direct challenge to the heterosexual norm, was also ignored for centuries. The early beginnings of recognizing the clitoris did nothing but mask it further by equating it with the penis. We all know Freud's theory of the tomboy for whom the female genitals take the form of an absence. As the scar of castration, the clitoris would be women's disabled penis. Again, but in his own unique way, Freud is a prisoner of the unisex model. In a bold thesis, *Making Sex: Body and Gender from the Greeks to Freud,*[5] Thomas Laqueur argues that, from antiquity up to the eighteenth century, the dominant conception was that of a single sex in which the anatomical differences between men and women were viewed as insignificant. According to this model, there was but a single sex organ: female sexual organs were found inside the body, while male sexual organs were outside of it. The late anatomical discovery of the clitoris did nothing to disarm this schema.

Hence the fantastical fabrication of the lesbian and the male invert, subsequently torn apart by Simone de Beauvoir.[6]

Even construed as a maimed penis, the clitoris has always been associated with excessive pleasure. It is of no use whatsoever to reproduction. Erased, but lascivious. Legend tells of certain gorgons endowed with a voluminous clitoris, condemned to masturbate in perpetuity. Ablation of the clitoris, or clitoridectomy, was seen as a therapeutic means of castrating a woman a second time by calming her passions. It's a radical solution to infinite pleasure.

Excision exists in all cultures, not just in Africa as is too often assumed. In the West, it was employed as a therapy for hysterics and nymphomaniacs. There are several ways to cut the clitoris – physically, of course, since there's also a whole range of psychic excisions. That legendary frigidity – the opposite of nymphomania – is but one.

Absence, ablation, mutilation, denial. Can the clitoris exist in our minds, bodies and unconscious in any other mode than the negative?

*

They say things have changed. True enough. The anatomical, symbolic, political life of the clitoris is celebrated today from a wide range of perspectives, cultures, practices, activism and performance. As Nadya Tolokonnikova from the group Pussy Riot puts it in her rallying call, "Rise up for the clit revolution!"

Happily, many books have been published recently decrying the invisibility of the clitoris.[7] A whole new geography, aesthetic and ethic of pleasure is asserting itself – one that is a far cry from the heterosexual matrix and that can be summarized in just two words: "beyond penetration."[8]

The lines are also being redrawn within feminism. The discourse has undergone a radical transformation from second- and third-wave feminism to ultra-contemporary transfeminism. It is no longer – or not solely – a matter of designating the clitoris as the exclusive mark of women. For queer, intersexual and trans approaches, the clitoris has become the name of a libidinal disposition that does not necessarily belong to women, thereby reworking traditional views of sexuality, pleasure and gender. Alternative surgeries, alternative fantasies. From now on, exclaims Paul B. Preciado, there's no exclusive or universal model and we can – everyone can – light up "a clitoris on the solar plexus."[9]

And yet . . .

*

The reason I'm writing this book is that it seems nothing has really changed. Sexual mutilations are common practice, still. Pleasure is off-limits for millions of women, still. And still today the clitoris remains the physically and psychically erased pleasure organ. Also, doesn't dismissing one form of erasure inevitably amount to erasing it otherwise? Isn't to recognize one reality simultaneously to misrecognize it differently? Isn't shedding light always an act of violence? Stroking with one hand, rubbing out with the other.

*

Of course, the history of the clitoris can also be read as a linear trajectory, a history of progress, leading from erasure to visibility, deletion to existence. Finally, now, the clitoris has achieved some respect, at least in some countries and contexts. However, at each stage, each step in this "progress," yawns an abyss. It's not enough to celebrate the existence of the clitoris, describe its anatomy in detail, highlight its importance, engage it in a performative affirmation, to put an end to this eclipse. All my reading, all my research has led me to conclude that to touch the clitoris – in a figurative sense, and perhaps too in reality – is always, on every occasion, to experience a *caesura*. The clitoris exists only within this caesura, which compromises neither its autonomy nor its orgasmic intensity, but also, paradoxically, does make it difficult to view as complete, unified, sufficient to itself.

The caesura between clitoris and vagina has been the object of so many analyses, so many psychoanalyses. Then there's the caesura between clitoris and penis. And the caesura between clitoris and phallus, since, unlike the penis, the clitoris refuses to obey the law of the phallus. The caesura between biology and symbol, flesh and meaning. Also, the caesura between feminism's "subjects," and thus between feminisms too. Caesurae between bodies. The caesura between the anatomical determination of sex and the social plasticity of gender. The caesura between birth body and surgical interventions. The caesura between claiming the existence of "woman" and the rejection of "woman" as a category. The caesura between "we women" and a multiplicity of experiences that prevent the unifying or universalizing of this same "we" and these "women."

The caesura is not only difference – difference between same and other, or difference from the self. Difference – including sexual difference – is just one instance of a caesura. The caesura fractures the paradoxical identity of difference by revealing the multiplicity it shelters.

Of course, it's somewhat surprising that *one* organ, *one* part of the body, *one* part of the genitals – the clitoris – should claim to account for so many caesurae. Why privilege the clitoris itself over other zones, including those that are not necessarily genital?

Because it's a silent symbol.

Let's start with the fact that only a handful of philosophers have ever dared to mention the clitoris, even though the work of these male thinkers is filled with references to other parts of women's bodies – breasts, vagina, labia. The phallocracy of philosophical language is no longer a mystery. After naming "phallocentrism" and "phallogocentrism,"[10] Jacques Derrida set about deconstructing this language through a critique of its main characteristics: the privileging of rectitude, erection (the architectural model of all that stands), visibility, the phallus as symbol and the concurrent reduction of woman to matrix-matter, mother, vagina–uterus. But on woman's pleasure in philosophy – not a word.

In *The History of Sexuality*, Michel Foucault devotes not a single line to the clitoris, except to describe the "monstrous" clitoris of a hermaphrodite.[11] Aside from that, at no point does he ever consider the clitoris' role in the "use of pleasures."[12] Perhaps that's because, when it comes to the clitoris, it would be difficult to challenge the "repressive hypothesis" . . .[13]

From its origins, and still today, Western philosophical discourse is governed by phallogocentrism.

For all that, one of philosophy's tasks, in terms of both research and ethics, has always been to shed light on areas of life that, for one reason or another, remain hidden, buried or repressed. To name the clitoris in philosophy is to bring it into sight. But how can this be achieved without shading it again? If philosophical language is itself a logical excision, how can the clitoris be thought?

A second point to consider is that those women philosophers who tried to resolve this contradiction by bringing the clitoris into thought have been criticized, if not downright ridiculed, by third- and fourth-wave feminists. In *The Second Sex*, which is widely and quite rightly considered a philosophical work, Beauvoir dared confront clitoris with concept by openly discussing women's "two sexual organs," as well as the distinctiveness of a pleasure that is not necessarily linked to reproduction. But her approach was deemed essentialist, too invested in exploring an assumed identity of woman.

After sexual difference, other theories appeared, criticizing the fixity of gender, nature and binaries. They opened, and continue to open wide, other caesurae, between philosophy and politics, dominant and minoritized languages, Eurocentrism and decolonial approaches. As a result, the clitoris was deprived of its simple status as a "genital organ" that was woman's privilege. What is the clitoris – a masculine noun in French, feminine in Italian, ungendered in a non-Romance language such as English – for a non-binary subject, *they*, someone who identifies as neither man nor woman? Isn't it time, Delphine Gardey rightly asks, to free ourselves of the "fetishizing of organs and anatomy, the focus on physiology?" As she points out, "that's what Judith Butler suggests . . . by questioning the conception of the body and the erotics at play in the production of the body in terms of 'parts.'"[14]

But haven't these new developments in sexuality, gender and bodies – necessary as they are – produced their own form of erasure?

Why must we stop painting the portrait of the clitoris just as it appears, its ink still wet, so to speak? Why must we tag texts by Simone de Beauvoir and Luce Irigaray, or radical Italian feminists such as Carla Lonzi and Silvia Federici, as irredeemably outdated? Why not listen again to those who first dared let the clitoris speak?

The position I am assuming here is that of a radical feminist situated at a distance from the terfs (trans-exclusionary radical feminists) – that is, those who claim that trans activism makes the specific fights for women's rights invisible and inaudible.[15] I am certainly not among those who think that sexual binaries are written in stone and who deplore what they consider to be the excesses of gender theory, condemn same-sex parenting and continue making concessions to phallocracy.

But, at the same time, I cannot support the systematic dismissal of feminists from before gender, the founders of radical feminism who have been thrown aside.

Still, today, the clitoris bears the trace of a wound against which words wash up like waves, pulling away as soon as they emerge. This is not to say that it is the place of a lack, of the signifier, the letter or object a, b, c or z. It's far more complicated than that, and also far simpler. Even if it is not necessarily a woman's clitoris, the clitoris remains the mysterious place of the feminine. Which means it still hasn't found its place.

In a series of brush-strokes, I have sketched out its place here, a composite of simultaneous revelation and disappearance, cut each from another, drawn from different discourses, without hierarchy or judgment. The chapters may be read in order, following a timeline of feminism, or randomly, in which case they loop back on each other.

I'm not trying to prove anything; I seek instead to amplify diverse voices and to find a balance through them between the extreme difficulty and extreme urgency of speaking the feminine today.

Consider my strokes as so many small clitorises. Without representing it, my writing depicts the status of a pleasure organ that, even as a *scruple*, has yet to become an organ for thought.

2

Nymphs 1
Virtual Goddesses

The two labia minora are called nymphs, because they are said to direct the flow of urine, . . . they lie either side of the upper half of the vulva inside the labia majora.

(Georges Cuvier, *Leçons d'anatomie comparée*, V, 1805, p. 122)

"Nymph" has two meanings. Firstly, nymphs are mythological divinities. Secondly, in French, "nymphs" refers to the labia minora of the vulva and is often erroneously used as a synonym for "clitoris." What does this confusion conceal?

*

Who are the nymphs?

Homeric mythology represents the Nymphs as goddesses (θεαί) with a lower status than the Olympian deities, who do, however, welcome them into their midst for deliberations on important matters. Daughters of Jupiter, Nymphs live on earth and shelter in the woods or on mountain peaks, near springs, or in meadows and caves. In the *Iliad* and *Odyssey*, they accompany Diana, circling the goddess with their dances, watching over the fate of humans, planting trees, presiding over the hunt; sacrifices were made to them, either in special ceremonies, or together with Mercury.[1]

The most well-known image of nymphs presents them as gracious maidens, bright forces of nature, virtual goddesses.

While nymphs are most often represented as wild creatures, pursued by satyrs, sometimes they are represented instead as the feminine version of satyrs – the maenads – famous for their endless erotic adventures. Hence the subsequent neologism "nymphomania."

Since, as a result of an anatomical error, what was in fact the clitoris was termed nymph, henceforth nymphomaniac referred to a creature whose clitoris was on fire.

In between mythological nymphs – be they well behaved or debauched – and anatomical nymphs, there's also the nymphet, Nabokov's invention for his Lolita: "Between the age limits of nine and fourteen there occur maidens who, to certain bewitched travelers, twice or many times older than they, reveal their true nature . . . and these chosen creatures I propose to designate as 'nymphets.'"[2]

As an immature creature, the nymphet, that contemporary figure of the mythological nymph, is reminiscent of the state of an insect transforming, in the intermediary stage between larva and adult, which is also known as nymph, or nymph stage. As a disarmingly charming, provocative young girl, she kindles desire due to her synonymy with what is hidden between her labia – both threatening and attractive – and whose name is silenced.

There is one feature that all these nymphs, nymphets and nymphomaniacs share: supposedly, they never attain pleasure. Pleasure remains captive of the chrysalis.

And since the nymph never comes, she's the

erotic phantasy *par excellence*. The ideal woman is then she who is without a clitoris.

Allow me to begin by taking a short detour to analyze this erasure.

3

Nymphs 2
Images without Genitals

Agamben, Boccaccio, Warburg

In his slim volume, *Nymphs*,[1] Giorgio Agamben unveils the true nature of the nymph: she's an image.

Agamben takes us on a fascinating voyage through time, starting with Bill Viola, reaching back to Boccaccio and ending with Aby Warburg. En route, he asks what is the origin of the infamous caesura between the image of woman (muse, nymph) and real woman? From the time when it was a central feature of medieval poetry, this caesura has never ceased to govern the Western imaginary, to the point that still today it haunts contemporary art.

In Boccaccio's texts, the nymph "is the preeminent love object"[2] precisely because she is an image. The beloved, carried everywhere by the lover, hidden in a jewel or purse, painted in a portrait or hidden in a poem or a coat of arms, is desirable precisely because she has lost her body. The lover can therefore interiorize her, keep her in his thoughts. The nymph is woman become idea. For Boccaccio, the quintessence of this idea is the Florentine nymph.

The nymph accommodates a fundamental ambiguity: the simultaneous unity and disunity of the fantasy of woman and woman herself. Like the emerging insect, she is midway between larva and full life. "If the *ninfale* is that poetic dimension in which the images . . . should coincide with real women, then the *ninfa fiorentina* is always-already in the process of dividing herself according to her opposed polarities – at once too alive and too inanimate – while the poet no longer succeeds in granting her a unified existence."[3] Due to its ambivalence, the nymph-image is thus "a sublime . . . rupture," taking place "between the sensible world and thought," the birth place of literature. She offers the aura of the real, its fantastic dimension, forever unfinished. Image and living body can never be one. Indeed, the image has no genitals.

Paracelsus places the nymph in the "doctrine of the elemental spirits (or spiritual creatures), each of whom is connected to one of the four elements: the nymph (or undine) to water, the sylphs to air, pygmies (or gnomes) to earth, and salamanders to fire."[4] These creatures are just like human creatures, they resemble them physically, but the fundamental difference is that they "have no soul."[5] Larval, they are not yet entirely living, for "It is only in the encounter with man that the inanimate images acquire a soul."[6] To come to life and leave the image, nymphs must consummate the romantic relationship.

Yet this consummation remains forever impossible. How can one make love to an image? The nymphs "are ladies," as Boccaccio writes, "they have their outward semblance."[7] They look like them but they are missing something . . . Boccaccio conjures up a new image here: "It is quite true they are all females, but they don't *piss*."[8]

Since the muse-nymph has neither soul nor real body, she is also deprived of . . . well, what exactly? Because the inadequate anatomy of the time made no real distinction between clitoris, labia, vagina and uterus, Boccaccio reduces the vulva to urination. "Nymphs" are women who "don't piss."[9] Agamben concludes that this phrase demonstrates Boccaccio's "brusque realism."[10]

Really? Realism? If it's the case that nymphs come to life solely by joining sexually with a man, would copulation animate them by making them urinate? Realism? This confusion between pissing and coming? That's exactly what "nymphs don't piss" means: they don't come. They have no genitals until man turns up. And in the male imagination, these genitals are endowed with a fantastical anatomy.

No surprise then that Boccaccio develops a "ferocious critique of women," preferring nymphs to them, since nymphs are less moody, less threatening.

What about several centuries later? What does Agamben himself think, for instance? Have the clitoris and vulva gone back to their places? Has real woman reclaimed her rights?

Agamben only mentions the anatomical meaning of nymphs in a brief parenthetical comment when he refers to nymphomania in passing. Returning to Paracelsus, he writes: "Paracelsus is connecting with another, more ancient, tradition that indissolubly tied the nymphs to amorous passion and the reign of Venus (this tradition lies at the origin of both the psychiatric term 'nymphomania' and, perhaps, also of the anatomical term *nymphaea*, the small lips of the vulva)."[11]

Nymphaea also refers to the clitoris. But not a word on that either from Agamben.

The nymph is thus confused with the absence of the clitoris, which is never named or recognized in its reality – that is, according to the precise morphology of female genitals. "The Mount of Venus,"[12] so dear to Paracelsus, hides the enigma of an eclipse.

Later, the great German art historian Aby Warburg gave further life to this enigma when he named one of the "pathos formulae" (*Pathosformeln*) "nymph." These "pathos formulae" are the passionate gesture languages "of Western humanity."[13] Warburg collated the archetypes in his *Mnemosyne Atlas*, which he worked on consistently from 1921 to 1929. In the *Atlas*, "Nymph" is *Pathosformel* number 46. This number accompanies a plate which "contains twenty-six photographs, starting from a seventh-century Longobard relief to a fresco by Domenico Ghirlandaio in Santa Maria Novella."[14] Agamben asks: "Where is the nymph? In which one of the table's twenty-six apparitions does it reside? To search among them for an archetype or an original from which the others have derived would amount to misreading the *Atlas*."[15]

The nymph is everywhere and nowhere, she traverses all these wide-ranging phenomena, which are, strictly speaking, her imaginary or imagined being, and still does not run dry. Yet this abundance tells us nothing at all about the burning place between her thighs. Warburg says not a thing about her genitals. The nymphs of the nymph are never named. Not a word on nymphomania. Nothing about desire. No word about the labia, or about the clitoris they shelter. Not a word on pleasure. The image is even more abstract here than in Boccaccio. Their life is now nothing but a "historical" life: "We are used to attributing life only to the biological body. Instead, a purely historical life is one that is *ninfale*."[16] Thus Agamben concludes, with this lack of conclusion.

When they called the clitoris "nymph," did anatomists have a specific idea of what they were referring to? Wasn't the vulva for them what it no doubt remains for many of our contemporaries – especially philosophers – namely, the hazy origin of pleasure, reproduction and urination all at once? No doubt life is not solely the privilege of biological bodies. But if this is the case, then those bodies can't be deprived of biological life.

4

Nymphs 3
Nadja, or a Being without Life

A Brief Commentary on
"The Woman Love Object"

I certainly would not have read Agamben's text in the same way if Simone de Beauvoir had not alerted my suspicions about this nymph of writers and poets in her incisive analysis of "the woman love object" in *The Second Sex*. "The woman love object" is at the heart of the chapter on "Myths" in which she establishes the close connection between mythology and mystery, mystery and mystification. Both the mythology of the nymph and the mystery of the image of woman are expressions of the masculine fantasy of sculpting. The nymph is a malleable matter that man shapes as he sees fit, as Beauvoir explains: "One of the daydreams he enjoys is the impregnation of things by his will, shaping their form, penetrating their substance: the woman is par excellence the 'clay in his hands' that passively lets itself be worked and shaped."[1] As an "image" of woman, the nymph is the result of this kind of shaping. The Muse too is none other. "The Muses are women,"[2] writes Beauvoir, but improved women since they neither piss nor come – in other words, they actually have no autonomy. "The Muse creates nothing on her own."[3]

Beauvoir then proposes readings of poets who fall in love with their nymphs. I was particularly struck by the example of André Breton. Enraptured by *Nadja*'s beauty, I had never noticed the extent to which Breton remains faithful to the nymph tradition in this book.[4] For him, Nadja resembles the mythological nymph: "a free genius, something like one of those spirits in the air."[5] Yet, as Beauvoir rightly comments, "she opens the doors to the surreal world: but she is unable to give it."[6] She is at best "an oracle one questions."[7] "Woman deprived of her human base,"[8] "child-woman,"[9] she becomes a poet . . . thanks only to the poet.

We follow each manifestation in turn and dive into the undine that gradually emerges in the waves of writing as her Pygmalion shapes her, and in so doing has his pleasure. For her, however, there will be no pleasure. Not a word on it. Poetry comes to a stop at the threshold of her excitation. The nymph, the Muse, is "All except herself."[10] While "her only vocation is love,"[11] no one thinks to ask whether she herself is, in fact, in love – whether her body is implicated in this erotic game. Whether seeing herself loved in words and images offers the satisfaction of her pleasure.

Nymph poetry, even of the surrealist sort, thus sometimes serves to gag the supposedly beloved chrysalis.

From January 1928 to August 1932, the Surrealists engaged in a game of sexual truth telling. Breton would ask his friends provocative questions such as: "To what extent does Aragon believe that erection is necessary for the sexual act?" or "Does Marcel Noll know where the clitoris is?"[12]

Breton certainly did know where it was but he did not subject it to this truth-telling exercise, nor did he give it the chance to speak.

The nymphs of philosophers and poets are bound, all of them, in the same dark night of silence.

5

Political Anatomy

Back to reality. All female mammals have a clitoris. Among quadrupeds, it is situated near the vagina and is therefore stimulated by penetration. Coupling stimulates orgasm and ovulation simultaneously. In the words of biologist Pierre-Henri Gouyon: "The arrangement of ovulatory mechanisms in mammals today ... suggests that ovulation caused by copulation is the original model."[1] In the course of evolution, "as a result of the vertical straightening of the pelvis, the clitoris became an anterior organ, visible and accessible from the front."[2] In women, the clitoris is thus not – or rather, is no longer – positioned at the entrance to the vagina. It has moved away from it. Spontaneous ovulation, occurring autonomously and cyclically without the need for any sexual relation, is a belated evolutionary innovation. Unlike male orgasm, female orgasm has no direct function in reproduction: "After having played a major role in ovulation, it has largely lost this function among women and now offers nothing but pleasure."[3]

There is a caesura, a space between clitoris and vagina. But is this just an anatomical fact? If such were the case, wouldn't we know more about orgasm in general – including animal orgasm, about which we know next to nothing? The specific question of female orgasm makes the point in a particularly telling manner: biology and politics are indistinguishable. Indeed, the debates about the caesura between clitoris and vagina, orgasm and reproduction, in fact obscure the issue of the autonomy of women's pleasure. Is there a being then that can enjoy sexual pleasure without bearing children? Is there a pleasure then that exists *for no reason*? By what right does the sole mammal that can claim this pleasure do so? The fact that this exception is acknowledged does not mean that it is accepted. The autonomy of woman's pleasure has – and perhaps will always have – to be debated, defended, constructed.

The continuous raging arguments over whether female sexual pleasure exists independently from reproduction are proof enough. In a suggestively titled article, "The Truth about the Clitoris: Why It's Not Just Built for Pleasure," British journalist Zoe Williams wrote: "The results are finally in – a study in *Clinical Anatomy* has found that the clitoris does play an important role in reproduction, activating a series of brain effects . . .: enhancement of vaginal blood flow, increased lubrication, oxygen and temperature, and an altered position of the cervix, which paradoxically slows down the sperm and improves their motility."[4] Apparently, the logic of adaptive evolution has lost none of its claims in the matter. By all means necessary, female pleasure will be brought back to a purported "function."

The theoretical privileging of the clitoris over other parts of the vulva, and over the vulva itself, along with its metonymic fetishizing, can be explained by the fact that it symbolizes the independence of this pleasure. It becomes the major element that allows us to construct female sexuality, to view women as sexual subjects on their own terms, "no longer married . . . to the penis or the law."[5] To reduce pleasure to reproductive purposes once again is to deny it.

Yet positive recognition of the autonomy of the clitoris has also been a source of anxiety and conflict. Some women have wondered what can be done when there is no vaginal pleasure or when the clitoris becomes *too* independent, condemning woman to remaining "cold" during penetration. Psychoanalyst Marie Bonaparte's remedy to her own frigidity was to have recourse to surgery. Believing that her clitoris was too far from her vagina, in 1927 she asked a Viennese doctor, Professor Halban, to resituate her clitoris. Since still she found no pleasure, in 1930 and 1931 she underwent two further surgeries. Still nothing. Nonetheless, she continued to maintain that among women in general, the distance – that caesura – between the two organs is excessive. She argued this point in her article "Considérations sur les causes anatomiques de la frigidité chez la femme," published under the pseudonym A. E. Narjani. The study discusses a sample of "two hundred women chosen at random among the Parisian population," whose "small triangular area" was carefully measured in order to determine the distance between this area and the vagina.[6] "The problem of women's frigidity is still shrouded in great mystery," she wrote, "And yet, in all places and at all times we hear the moan of women who even the deepest caress of love fails to satisfy."[7]

Through her experiments, Bonaparte sought to convince Freud, "the great exciser," that it was impossible to renounce the clitoral phase. Freud believed that the normal sexual evolution of women involved giving up the clitoral stage of pleasure in favor of the vaginal stage, thereby aligning with the reproductive function of sexuality. Despite her own bodily experiences, Bonaparte replied that there was no orgasm without the clitoris and that, on its own, the vagina remained silent. So why not try to artificially grant the unresponsive vagina something of the burning ardor of the clitoris without waiting for an improbable maturing? Freud ignored her. The surgical intervention thus did nothing but underscore the erasure of pleasure.

It's impossible to bridge the caesura.

6

"Sexual Existence" according to Simone de Beauvoir

The vulva made its appearance in philosophy for the first time ever in *The Second Sex*. Sexuality had been granted the dignity of a category of thought in Jean-Paul Sartre's *Being and Nothingness*, published originally in 1943, which shed light on the as yet unexplored relation between sexuality and existence. As Sartre argued:

> existential philosophies have not believed it necessary to concern themselves with sexuality. Heidegger, in particular, does not make the slightest allusion to it in his existential analytic with the result that his *Dasein* appears to us as asexual. Of course one may consider that it is contingent for "human reality" to be specified as "masculine"

and "feminine"; of course one may say that the problem of sexual differentiation has nothing to do with that of *Existence* (*Existenz*) since man and woman equally exist. These reasons are not wholly convincing.[1]

Sartre thus devotes many long pages to desire, mentioning in passing "the erection of the penis and the clitoris" and positing that, far from being a "contingent accident," sexuality is "a necessary structure of being-for-itself-for-others."[2]

Although Beauvoir praises the remarkable advance offered by Sartre's analysis, she identifies a major problem within it: how does this conceptualization of sexuality avoid still leading to a disembodiment? After all, in Sartre's conception, sexuality is none other than a new version of the Hegelian dialectic known as master and slave. Reading Maurice Merleau-Ponty served only to heighten her concern. In *Phenomenology of Perception*, he too placed sexuality in the realm of battle. Writing about nudity during the sexual act, Merleau-Ponty explained "Shame and immodesty . . . take their place in a dialectic of the self and the other which is that of master and slave."[3]

How should these statements be interpreted? Even as they assert the importance of sexuality, existentialist philosophers view it as the expression of a dilemma, a conflict between freedom and desire. Sartre claims "Man cannot be sometimes slave and sometimes free; he is wholly and forever free or he is not free at all."[4] The problem is that desire reintroduces necessity into the absolute freedom of existence. As Hegel demonstrated, desire is necessarily alienating since it always tends toward the appropriation of the other, their transformation into a thing, their consumption and annihilation: "It is not enough merely that troubled disturbance should effect the Other's incarnation: desire is the desire to appropriate this incarnated consciousness. Therefore desire is naturally continued not by *caresses* but by acts of taking and of penetration."[5]

Beauvoir sees right away that, while in theory the Other applies to both sexes, woman is more often slave than master in this game of desire. Moreover, she is a slave who evokes disgust and terror. Sartre writes:

The obscenity of the feminine sex is that of everything which "gapes open." It is an *appeal to being* as

all holes are. In herself woman appeals to a strange
flesh which is to transform her into a fullness of
being by penetration and dissolution. Conversely
woman senses her condition as an appeal, precisely
because she is "in the form of a hole."[6]

Refuting these pronouncements unequivocally,
Beauvoir makes the decisive move by displacing the
phenomenological–existential study of sexuality –
the approaches of both Sartre and Merleau-Ponty
– toward a "philosophy of sexual existence"[7] – that
is, a philosophy of lived sexuality that thoroughly
reexamines the question of the desiring body.
Instead of abandoning phenomenology – in other
words, the rigorous description of beings and
things not as they are but as they appear – Beauvoir
transforms it. Sexuality cannot be understood
without first acknowledging that it too is a phenomenon, a manifestation. Sexing – which today
we would call gender formation – does not occur
once and for all; rather, it takes place throughout
a life in a series of successive appearances of the
body to itself and to others. There is no sexed
body, only sexual embodiment.

While this process cannot be the same for both
sexes, this in no way implies an inevitable battle

to the death. Of course, Beauvoir does not decon-struct the gender binary, but she does deploy it as an instrument of resistance – resistance to the concept of an "Other" that is still too uniformly masculine. As she writes, "It has already been said here that man never thinks himself without thinking the Other; he grasps the world under the emblem of duality . . . But being naturally different from man, who posits himself as the same, woman is consigned to the category of Other; the Other encompasses woman."[8] The whole purpose of *The Second Sex* is thus to free woman from the weight of the alterity that erases her singularity.

Beauvoir presents the genesis of the sexual bodily incorporation of woman and connects her morphology to her becoming-subject. The famous statement "One is not born, but rather becomes, woman"[9] is a response to what Sartre analyzes as an ahistorical fact: female anatomy for him gapes open as an incomplete lack. Beauvoir objects: no, woman's body has its own plenitude since it appears to itself through the varied rhythm of its different forms. Her sexual organ is a figure that emerges and is refined through a series of sketches, in collusion with the mirror. The sketch of the child, the young girl, the mature woman, the old woman. Youth, maturity, old age are not mere facts – rather, they are modes of existence. While in English one "is" a given age, in French they say one "has" such and such an age, but that one "is" young or old, and this "being" coincides with the way in which the body speaks to the world and the way the world responds. By contrast, to be "in the form of a hole" would be to belong to no world, to simply *not exist*. Moreover, desire is not fundamentally murderous or alienating. Desire is the reverberation, the shimmering of the constitution of a body. Beauvoir did what had to be done by gently nudging sexuality toward eroticism. In so doing, she recognized the role of the forgotten one, the clitoris.

This type of existential erotics must involve a critique of Freud. Beauvoir writes: "Freud was not very concerned with woman's destiny; it is clear that he modeled his description of it on that of masculine destiny, merely modifying some of the traits."[10] Moreover, he declares that "the libido is constantly and regularly male in essence, whether in man or in woman." This means that he "refuses to posit the feminine libido in its originality."[11] According to Freud, woman is a mutilated man, as she was also later for Sartre. To repeat: for them, the clitoris is, and is only ever, a miniature penis. Reduced, cut, castrated.

Beauvoir rejects these assertions outright. She contests the descriptors "vaginal" and "clitoral" on her own terms, explaining that the "categories clitoral or vaginal, like the categories bourgeois and proletarian, are equally inadequate to encompass a concrete woman."[12] However, *The Second Sex* still runs up against the duality of feminine pleasure: "one of the great problems of female eroticism is that clitoral pleasure is localized: it is only in puberty, in connection with vaginal eroticism, that many erogenous zones develop in the woman's body."[13] While clitoral pleasure does not disappear and while it is an unavoidable, irreducible manifestation of bodily incorporation, it is not truly realized except through its relation with vaginal pleasure, to which it must ultimately cede supremacy.

The Second Sex is deeply indebted to *Psychoanalysis of the Sexual Functions of Women* (1947), written by Helene Deutsch, the Polish psychoanalyst who immigrated to the United States and who was an orthodox Freudian.[14] Beauvoir, who refers to this work on several occasions,[15] shares Deutsch's idea that the complexity of female sexuality lies in the relation between the two organs. For both Beauvoir and Deutsch – as for Freud – this relation can only be one of progress. Deutsch returns to the idea of the female castration complex due to "the absence of an organ."[16] As a result, for the young girl, "the inhibited activity accepts the turn towards passivity" – in other words, the clitoris, which is the active organ, must accept the paradoxical domination of the passive organ, the vagina. Hence her definition of the "feminine woman": "If the woman succeeds in establishing this maternal function of the vagina by renouncing the claim of the clitoris to be a penis surrogate, she has completed the development to womanhood."[17]

Losing one's virginity certainly does not always produce the anticipated pleasure, as Beauvoir comments. "Here we reach the crucial problem of feminine eroticism":[18] the beginning of erotic life is necessarily clitoral, prior to its vaginal future, the pleasure that supposedly emerges with penetration. And yet:

it has been seen that defloration is not a successful accomplishment of youthful eroticism; it is on the contrary an unusual phenomenon; vaginal pleasure is not attained immediately; according to Stekel's statistics – confirmed by many sexologists and psychoanalysts – barely 4 percent of women experience pleasure at the first coitus; 50 percent do not reach vaginal pleasure for weeks, months, or even years. Psychic factors play an essential role in this.[19]

Additionally, "Man's attitude is thus of extreme importance."[20] If he is violent or too rough in his desire, the vaginal orgasm will not occur. As a result, "Resentment is the most common source of feminine frigidity."[21] Yet, apparently, if all goes well, if a man is patient and understanding, the transfer of power between the two organs will take place successfully . . .

It would be wrong, however, to equate Beauvoir's analyses with those of Deutsch. Beauvoir construes the relation between clitoris and vagina as a political relation, an expression of inequality between a subject who has two organs and a subject who has only one. In patriarchal societies, it is a privilege to have just one. That's why woman feels obligated to abandon one of hers. Her critique of this situation is damning. Yet there is a discrepancy in Beauvoir's work between the political thrust of her arguments and her view of female anatomy. The clitoris and vagina still play their traditional roles even as the critical reflection transgresses them.

How is it possible to remove the division between clitoral activity and vaginal passivity, between pleasure and reproduction? How does the relation of commanding to obeying play out between thought and sexuality?

Has Beauvoir not reintroduced the master and slave relation she wanted to exclude from sexuality into the very core of female intimacy?

Philosophy and psychoanalysis simultaneously offer a resource and an obstacle. There is no feminism that has not had, or still does not have, to clear a path both with and against them. With unparalleled intelligence, *The Second Sex* bears witness to the barrenness of this undertaking.

7

Dolto, Lacan and the "Relationship"

> It is of utmost importance that the girl "stops mourning" her clitoral masturbatory fantasies . . . The happy solution is vaginal investment.
>
> (Françoise Dolto, *Psychoanalysis and Paediatrics: Key Psychoanalytical Concepts with Sixteen Clinical Observations of Children*, trans. Françoise Hivernel and Fiona Sinclair, London: Karnac, 2013, p. 78)

Let's take a moment to consider women psychoanalysts. Can we even imagine today the difficulty they faced trying to speak publicly about feminine sexuality before the last century's famed sexual liberation? I try to picture an already older Françoise Dolto in 1960, filled with trepidation when Lacan entrusted her with the task of presenting a report on the subject at the Congress in Amsterdam. She complied with the request in a talk entitled "Sexualité féminine : la libido génitale et son destin féminin" [female sexuality: the feminine fate of genital libido].[1] She explained that both title and subtitle were imposed on her.

It's a long text. Her voice is muffled. Dolto is not entirely herself presenting this report. She's juggling, circling, dancing, tripping across a minefield: "I was asked to do this. In France, people were not yet ready to hear a report given by a woman."[2]

The Congress had been long in the making, with Lagache and Lacan preparing for it over two years. The text on these preparations, "Guiding Remarks for a Congress on Feminine Sexuality," was published in Lacan's *Écrits*.[3] The report Dolto gave covered the main points.

While the question of feminine sexuality had been at the heart of debates since the 1920s, in psychoanalysis it had led to nothing but a series of dead-ends. We might ask: has it even emerged from them now? It was up to Dolto to find a voice with which to wend her way through several theoretical constituencies already solidly in place. And she was to do so in the Société française de psychanalyse, which was rife with infighting.

There were at least four constituent groups. They were all – all four of them – crystallized or fossilized, around the infamous duo, those friends and foes: clitoris and vagina. Since Freud, the mysterious relation entertained by these two organs was, as he termed it, the "dark continent" of psychoanalysis. An oft-explored continent, it was one whose mystery remained intact.

The first constituency was Freud himself: sexual monism, the fundamentally masculine essence of the libido, the young girl's lack of awareness that her vagina exists, the fundamental role of the clitoris as a lesser counterpart to the penis, the construction of a phallic theory of sexuality. Then, around Freud, there was the second group associated with all of his disciples in Vienna, who shared his theses and adapted them to their own. Here we find Helene Deutsch, Jeanne Lampl de Groot, Ruth Mack Brunswick, Marie Bonaparte and Anna Freud. A third constituency gathered dissident disciples such as Karen Horney, Melanie Klein and Josine Müller in London, around Ernest Jones. Appealing to clinical observations, they countered Freud on the question of "penis envy." According to them, the nature of this envy is secondary and defensive. "Awareness of the vagina" is contemporaneous with clitoral desire. The young girl experiences it very early on, and the awareness cannot be reduced to passively waiting for the male.

And then finally, of course, comes the giant constituency that is Lacan. Retrospectively, we can see how remarks in *Seminar XIX . . . or Worse* reveal the context in which Dolto had to situate her talk – namely, contempt for feminism in general, and for Beauvoir in particular. A contempt that Lacan never sought to hide and of which he was apparently even proud.

In the seminar he mentions his failed encounter with Simone de Beauvoir:

> one famous author who . . . oriented by goodness knows what because in truth I hadn't started teaching anything yet, thought she should confer with me before delivering *The Second Sex*. She called me by phone to tell me that she would certainly need my advice in order to enlighten her as to what the psychoanalytic contribution of her book would be.[4]

But Lacan never did offer this "advice," as he explains:

> As I remarked to her that it would take at least a good five or six months for me to unravel the question for her – which is a minimum because I've been speaking about it now for twenty years, and this is not by chance – she announced that of course it was out of the question for a book that was already being finalized to have to wait so long, the laws of literary production being such that it seemed to her that having more than three or four consultations with me was impossible. Following which, I declined the honour.[5]

This refusal was not simply a matter of lack of time. Lacan fundamentally disagreed with the thesis summarized in the title of Beauvoir's book.

Why this disagreement? For Lacan, sexuality is not an exchange, a relation between two beings – rather, it is a function that obeys the law of language entirely. In the seminar he returns to his provocative statement: "Il n'y a pas de rapport sexuel"[6] – or there is no such thing as a sexual relationship.[7] The word "relationship" is perhaps more significant here than the word "sexual." "There is no sexual relationship" means, amongst other things, that man and woman are not destined for one another, oriented toward each other, as animals are, by a sexual instinct. In other words, to be a man or woman is not of the natural order. Boys and girls are different from "lion cubs," which, whether male or female, "look utterly alike in their behavior."[8] "But not you," Lacan continues, addressing his listeners, "precisely for as much as you sexuate yourselves *comme significant,* as signifying."[9] The difference between animals and humans lies in the fact that humans must speak about the sexual, write it, think about it, narrate it, fantasize about it. The discourse of love is fundamental to erotic experience. "The sexual relation must be reconstituted through discourse."[10] This need for discourse is precisely what erases the relational aspect of the sexual act, for two seemingly contradictory reasons. First, because this need is the same for both man and woman: sexual difference is annulled in discursive speech. Second, because although man and woman are subject to the same law of discourse, they do not understand one another when they speak. Thus, Lacan argues, between them there is no such thing as a "relationship."

Beauvoir's argument thus collapses when Lacan declares:

> *there is no second sex.* From the moment language starts functioning, there is no second sex. Or, to put it differently, concerning what is called hetero-sexuality, the word ἕτερος, which is the term that in Greek is used to say *other*, is in the position – for the relation that in the speaking being is called sexual – of emptying itself of its Being. This empti-ness which it offers to speech is precisely what I call the locus of the Other, namely the locus in which the effects of the said speech are inscribed.[11]

With these complex formulae, Lacan asserts that each sex constructs its own discourse, address-ing it to an Other who is not the other with whom they make love, but a total Other who is unknown, the true object of desire, to whom one speaks and who does not, and never will, cor-respond to the person who is physically present.

Lacan thus returns the second sex to the gener-alizing category of the Other from which Beauvoir had tried so hard to extract it. It is not that the categories of man and woman no longer mean anything, but they refer to the incommunicable

49

manners between them for relating to the same
language, for desiring the same absolute signifier. This signifier is the "phallus." Of course,
the phallus is not the penis, since, as we have
seen, sexuality infinitely exceeds the genitals. But,
despite everything, for both man and woman, the
phallus – the ultimate, master signifier of desire
– can only ever be an erection, a standing icon.
"The erect image of the phallus is what is crucial
here. There is only one. There is no other choice
but a virile image or castration."[12]

The symbol of the phallus is paradoxical for,
while its image is virile, it is not incarnated by
any sex. The autonomy of feminine sexuality,
the specificity of the relation between clitoris
and vagina, derive from this symbol and are not
therefore fundamental questions.

Already, in "Guiding Remarks for a Congress
on Feminine Sexuality," Lacan emphasized that
the question posed by the existence of the two
organs was both insoluble and pointless – as,
therefore, the two orgasms of woman are, too.
He writes:

The rather trivial opposition between clitoral jouissance and vaginal satisfaction [the distinction

between "jouissance" and "satisfaction" does not go unnoticed] has been so greatly reinforced by theory that it has worried many subjects, and the theory has even taken this worry up as a theme, if not as a demand – though we cannot say, for all that, that the opposition between them has been elucidated any more correctly. This is true because the nature of vaginal orgasm has kept its obscurity inviolate . . . Representatives of the fairer sex, however loud their voices among analysts, do not seem to have given their all to remove the seal . . . they have generally confined themselves to metaphors whose loftiness in the ideal signifies nothing preferable to what the hoi polloi give us by a way of a less intentional poetry.[13]

Lacan's rejection of the idea of the second sex joins, retrospectively, other disgraceful statements about women's inability to resolve their own question except through recourse to bad metaphors.

No second sex, no specifically feminine language, nothing to say about the clitoris or vagina, supremacy of the phallus; such is the straitjacket in which Dolto was trapped from the outset.

In fact, she herself deploys "metaphors," as she tries to slip personal reflections into the cracks between the different constituencies. These metaphors, which, admittedly, are more or less felicitous, include the clitoral "button" and vaginal "hole," which the young girl sometimes confuses "with the urinary orifice."[14] Dolto tries to have it all. From Freud, she takes the idea of an essentially masculine libido and the stages (from the pre-Oedipal phase to the Oedipal) that lead to vaginal pleasure. In Beauvoir, she respects the genealogical order of girl and woman from childhood to adolescence, from adolescence to adulthood, from maternity to menopause and old age. From the Jones group, she retains the theory of the young girl's early awareness of the existence of the vagina. And from Lacan, she maintains the thesis of the primacy of the phallus.

The first stage is the eros of the infant. The young girl "takes some time to find out how to 'take' her vulva."[15] Next comes the stage in which this taking is secured: "the girl pulls on her labia and 'button,' the clitoris; by exciting it she discovers its voluptuous erectility which, for some time, gives her hope that it is an emerging centrifugal penis."[16] The girl "imagines for herself a full, turgescent phallic form."[17] From the start, the young girl's sensations are vaginal and clitoral: she has a "button with a hole."[18]

The ensuing Oedipal phase occurs after a "narcissistic blow." It marks the shift from a "centrifugal" to a "centripetal" penis envy through a valorizing of cavities, as the prelude to reproductive desire.

Yet, of course, both penis and "button with a hole" obey the primacy of the phallus and, in this regard, Lacan obviously finds himself a powerful ally. Dolto accepts the idea that the sexual relationship paradoxically dissolves masculinity and femininity in the irreality of the phallus – the absolute signifier that, once again, no one ever incarnates or appropriates for themselves: "coitus is indeed a surrealist act in the full sense of the term, a 'derealization' that marks the loss for both man and woman of their common and complementary reference to the phallus."[19]

The only way for Dolto to make herself heard amongst the cacophony of all these mutually incompatible concessions is to draw on her experience as a clinician – notably, the testimonies she collected from children. Let the children speak, she says, since the symptoms they develop are reactions to all the sexual dysfunction of their parents. Children are echoes of adult libidos – echoes that usually go unheard by psychoanalysts. In fact, it is children who have the good sense to remind us of the bodily origin of sexuality, from which it has been distanced by too many signifiers. Dolto's power lies in the voice of children. Moreover, although her report was received with dead silence by the psychoanalysts of the time, it was widely appreciated by doctors, surgeons, obstetricians and gynecologists, many of whom requested a copy of the paper.

Lacan knew it, and on several occasions in his seminars he praised this aspect of her work. It did not escape him that the emphasis on children was the only truly original contribution of the report.

No doubt that's why, after the Congress and her reading of the report, he reportedly said to her: "Well, you've got a cheek to talk like that!"

Dolto recounted the exchange that followed. "I asked him: 'So, do you refute everything I said?' 'I didn't say that,' he answered, 'I said you've got a cheek.'" Dolto goes on, "Cheeky? What I said was certainly very different as a way to approach feminine sexuality, different from the approach of the men in the room who continued with the mindset typical of psychiatrists and philosophers."[20]

But how was this way of approaching feminine sexuality so very different? What part of it freed itself from dogma? In her book *Françoise Dolto : Une journée particulière*, Caroline Eliacheff presents several answers, each valid, dictated by listening to children.

> Was it because [Dolto] said that apparently heterosexual women were in fact homosexual in positioning their husband as their mother? Was it because she was talking about women acting perversely with their children yet not identified as pedophiles since maternal love justifies everything and anything? Was it because she claimed to have known women who were not frigid at all and who were completely nuts in the education they gave their children, at the time when it was believed that having orgasms was the panacea for all ills? Was it because she called out the inflation in the theory of the girl's disappointment upon discovering that she does not have a penis – a temporary disappointment from which she claimed the girl readily recovers?[21]

PLEASURE ERASED

What does a cheeky woman reveal? What does she conceal? All this, all at once? And, too, a new uncertainty about whether or not psycho-analysis is still relevant when it comes to feminine sexuality?

In response to the question asking what woman she herself was (which constituency she belonged to, what she was hiding), Dolto offered the following enigmatic response, an answer that is both naive and clever:

I really have no idea who I am and I'm very grateful to those who love and care for me because thanks to them, I can love and care for myself. But I'm entirely unsure who I am and that's why I can't answer you since I have no idea where my own femininity lies. I don't know, and it's impossible to talk about it.[22]

56

8

"The Feminine Sexual Organ is the Clitoris": Carla Lonzi and the Feminism of Difference

How do we transform, once and for all, an understanding of the relation between the two sexual organs, which all too often is considered in terms of a power relation?[1] How can we finally put an end to parsing the relation in terms of the old schema of mastery and servitude?

With Carla Lonzi, these questions resonate forcefully, clearing new ground like a forest fire. Born in Florence in 1931, Lonzi is one of the key figures of radical Italian feminism. Together with a group associated with La Libreria delle donne di Milano [the women's bookstore of Milan] in 1970, she founded the collective Rivolta Femminile [feminist revolt]. To devote herself to her cause, she left her partner and gave up her profession as a successful art critic. She abandoned her academic career and, despite the fact that it had been well received, refused to publish her thesis "Relations between the Stage and Visual Arts from the Late Nineteenth Century," written under the supervision of art historian Roberto Longhi. As Lonzi said, had she pursued this publication and career, "I would have been culturally 'categorized,' and that would have meant losing my one chance of having an identity."[2]

Lonzi was not trained as a philosopher, but her most celebrated work lies truly in the realm of the philosophical: *Sputiamo su Hegel!*, or *Let's Spit on Hegel!*, she exclaims in the title of her great manifesto.[3] As conceived by Hegel, the master and slave dialectic is a battle to the death. Two consciousnesses confront one another in a battle for recognition that demands a mutual face-off between their lives. To be recognized as consciousnesses instead of mere things, each must prove to the other that they have no attachment to life. Each must show themselves ready to die and, at the same time, ready to kill the other. Eventually, according to Hegel, one of the two consciousnesses gives in to fear and accepts submission to the other. One is master, the other slave. For Lonzi, this dialectic, with its oppositional logic, fails to account both for relations between men and women and for relations between vagina and clitoris – and, she insists, both relationships are inseparable from each other. Not that Lonzi is in denial of the violence that determines these relationships, since it is precisely the reality of masculine domination, along with its normalization of feminine sexuality, that she criticizes. The master and slave dialectic is mistaken on account of both origin and result. Lonzi writes:

> Had Hegel recognized the human origin of woman's oppression, as he did in the case of the slave's, he would have had to apply the master–slave dialectic in her case as well. But in doing so he would have encountered a serious obstacle. For, while the revolutionary method can capture the movement of the social dynamics, it is clear that woman's liberation could never be included in the same historical schemes. On the level of the woman–man relationship, there is no solution which eliminates the other; thus the goal of seizing power is emptied of meaning.[4]

The Hegelian conflict schema accepts the reality of taking power as its condition of possibility. Ultimately, the roles of master and slave may be reversed, but power remains intact. The task of feminism is thus to challenge the notion that power exists *a priori*. It's a matter of operating the lever that enables the simultaneous suspension and dislocation of submission and domination. And what exactly is this lever? *Difference.*

The concept of *difference*, as an alternative to oppositional logic, appeared for the very first time in *Let's Spit on Hegel!*

Faced with difference, the dialectic is futile. Feminism is not the thought of slaves freed.

Woman's difference is directly related to her sexuality, whose fundamental expression is the relationship between vagina and clitoris. We also have Lonzi to thank for the self-affirming clitoridian woman. In her other important manifesto, *The Clitoridian Woman and the Vaginal Woman*,[5] she asserts that the "clitoris must shed its secondary role."[6] There's no reason for it to be subjected to the power of the vagina since *it is the feminine sexual organ*: "The feminine sexual organ is the clitoris, the masculine sexual organ is the penis."[7]

On these grounds, the clitoris becomes

emblematic of the libidinal autonomy of woman – her difference – and so too the resistance zone to the hetero-normativity of "masculine sexual culture."

This gesture initiates a rupture with the traditional view of the two organs by taking apart the frequently proposed equivalence between clitoral sexual pleasure and masturbation. Even when shared with a partner – be they he or she – clitoral stimulation is often considered a form of auto-eroticism, "a pleasure experienced in a context of solitude and separation,"[8] thereby justifying its association with infantile activity. "Masculine sexual culture takes not only auto-eroticism, but any form of stimulation of sexual organs that is not coitus, to be masturbation."[9] Lonzi continues: "For this culture, clitoridian sexuality can only ever be practiced through masturbation, even when given by a partner."[10] By contrast, it is important to assert the clitoridian caress as an entirely other sexual relationship. "In my opinion, the difference between masturbation and non-masturbation lies in the perception of the presence of another person and in the erotic exchange, rather than in the fulfillment of a model of coitus"[11] – a model that is entirely

determined by "the ideological values of reproductive heterosexual penetration."[12]

The question of clitoridian orgasm is inseparable from the political question of subjectivization.
To proudly proclaim the clitoridian woman is
to launch a new becoming-subject. Lonzi establishes a defining relationship between clitoris and
thought when she declares that, for a woman, to be
clitoridian means "thinking in the first person."[13]
In fact, it is impossible to think by oneself without
knowing oneself, just as it is impossible to know
oneself without knowing where, or in what, one's
pleasure lies. In school, Lonzi writes, "young
people are taught how reproduction functions,
not about sexual pleasure."[14] If, for once, there is
a caesura that can be bridged, then it lies in the
under-examined caesura between knowing how
to think and knowing how to come. Between
knowing how one's mind is formed and knowing
how to lose one's mind.

Hence the concept of consciousness-raising
(*autocoscienza*). For a woman, self-consciousness
of her sex organ and pleasure is distinct from
consciousness of being this or that, vaginal or
clitoridian. It is not a matter of accepting a fact of
birth as inevitable. Consciousness-raising awak-

ens what it is consciousness of – namely the true source of desire. This is how it enables, firstly, putting an end to guilt over supposed vaginal frigidity. In fact, "vaginal woman" is only a projection of the masculine sexual schema, a fabrication of "patriarchal culture that has managed to keep the clitoris hidden and idle."[15] Lonzi continues, "How is it that the vaginal woman hesitates to become aware of such a vast sexual question?"[16] Precisely because patriarchal culture is a culture of clitoridectomy.

Clitoridian woman comes to represent feminine consciousness: "to fully enjoy clitoridian orgasm, woman must achieve psychic autonomy."[17] Laying claim to sexual difference is less about getting caught up in a binary schema than about deconstructing the concept of equality. Radical feminists do not look to be treated as equal to men, but rather to be considered as – and, first and foremost, to consider themselves as – what they are "authentically": that is, different. At the time, to recognize oneself as clitoridian was a true coming out. With "clitoridian woman," difference came out of the closet.

Obviously, for Lonzi, the critique of a heteronormative construction of feminine sexuality (the question of gender theory was not yet on the table) also involved a rejection of Freudian psychoanalysis, along with the association it makes between clitoris and immaturity, leaving women "vaginal aspirants."[18]

The refusal of Freudian psychoanalysis connects with the rejection of the Hegelian dialectic:

> For women, feminism takes the place of psychoanalysis for men. In psychoanalysis, man finds the reasons that make him unassailable ... In feminism, woman finds the collective feminine consciousness that develops the areas of her liberation. The category of repression in psychoanalysis is like that of the master and slave in Marxism [and Hegelianism]: together they form a patriarchal utopia in which woman is viewed as the very last human to be repressed and subjugated so as to support the massive effort of the masculine world in breaking the chains of repression and slavery.[19]

Henceforth, as the greatest stake in feminist consciousness-raising, the clitoris marks the irreducible caesura between subjection and responsibility.

Yet, how do women themselves avoid the reconstitution of phallic power? How do we bridge the caesura?

In her *Diaries*, Lonzi describes with poignancy the difficulties she encountered with her partner Ester, who felt dominated by her:

> With Ester I can only be quiet: she is mad at herself and she cannot take it; she blames her rage and her impotence on me. Now she says what she never said, what was unthinkable: that in my relationship to her I was the man and she was the woman. This is how the accusation of the vaginal to the clitoridian returns, and not even feminism will put an end to it.[20]

This expression of pessimism is all the more poignant since Lonzi did not live long enough to savor her victory in the power and popularity of what has been called, thanks to her and since her time, the "feminism of difference." This feminism is still being developed at the women's bookstore of Milan and in the Diotima Philosophical Community (Comunità Filosofica Diotima) at the University of Verona. Lonzi died in Milan on August 2, 1982, from cancer of the uterus, unaware that "sexual difference" would become, and remain for many years, the founding term of a new feminism.

9

Luce Irigaray: "Woman is neither Open nor Closed"[1]

The labia of the vulva – and lips of the mouth – are like guardians or gateways that harbor no power relation. Embedded between these lips, the clitoris and vagina are never rivals. As psychoanalyst and philosopher Luce Irigaray put it, "woman does not have sex organs. She has at least two of them, but they are not always identifiable as ones. Indeed, she has many more. Her sexuality, always at least double, goes even further: it is *plural*."[2]

This means that "women's pleasure does not have to choose between clitoral activity and vaginal passivity. . . . The pleasure of the vaginal caress does not have to be substituted for that of the clitoral caress. They each contribute, irreplaceably, to woman's pleasure."[3]

The complete absence of competition between the two sex organs is symbolized, intensified, by the relationship that exists between the lips themselves, which sit next to each other without any pressure. Deep in the secret of this sex organ that "touch[es] itself over and over again,"[4] between these lips (labia and mouth) that speak to each other, once again, there is "neither master nor slave."[5] Emerging as one of the dominant political problems of our time, here too sexual difference implies a break with the dialectic: "Each age has one issue to think through, and one only. Sexual difference is probably the issue in our time."[6] It bears repeating: this thought is not a thought based in conflict.

As she works incisively through a series of readings of Plato, Descartes, Hegel, Nietzsche and Heidegger, Irigaray refuses to define the fate of woman in philosophy as limited to mimesis, dooming her to ape men in the deployment of concepts. The thinking woman is not animated matter, a mere copy of the masculine *logos* that is always a form. Through an ironic and subversive mirror effect, woman diverts this mimesis and materiality. *Speculum* talks back to Lacan's mirror stage – that mirror that never reflects any woman. Of course, the title *Speculum of the Other Woman* references the gynecological instrument that makes it possible to "look *at the shadows*,"[7] but through an echo effect it also reveals that this darkness is in the eye of the beholder.

As they touch each other, the lips offer no glimpse of the mystery they shroud, if to be visible is taken to mean a prominent form that can be grasped by both eyes and hands. As for the "matter" that is supposedly the ontological part of the feminine, it is not without form, but "cannot be . . . formulated or *formalized*." "Woman is a common noun for which no identity can be defined. (The/a) woman does not obey the principle of self-identity."[8] Irigaray continues: "This self-touching gives woman a form that is in(de)finitely transformed without closing over her appropriation."[9] That which cannot be formed promises pleasure infinite metamorphoses.

In *This Sex which Is Not One*, Irigaray outlines a veritable geography of feminine pleasure. Even if the labia are in some sense the source of the libido, it is still the case that:

woman has sex organs more or less everywhere. She finds pleasure almost anywhere. Even if we refrain from invoking the hystericization of her entire body, the geography of her pleasure is far more diversified, more multiple in its differences, more complex, more subtle, than is commonly imagined – in an imaginary rather too narrowly focused on sameness. "She" is in(de)finitely other in herself.[10]

What criticism it elicited, Irigaray's articulation of woman and lips! And what skepticism this plural topography of pleasure has met! Whatever she says, Irigaray is accused of simplistically replacing phallomorphism with vulvomorphism, thereby signing off on her condemnation on account of essentialism! "Essentialism" is a poor word choice, however, since for the Greeks an essence (*eidos*) is movement, the dynamic of coming into presence or appearing. An essence, then, is anything but a nature or fixed instance. The fact that, through a subsequent metaphysical contraction, essence has become just that does not alter its originary plasticity. In fact, it seems that even Irigaray did not recognize the metamorphic nature of essence when she reduced it to the immobility of substance. To my mind, Irigaray is not essentialist enough.

Admittedly, her thought never goes beyond the theoretical matrix of sexual difference. There's the feminine and there's the masculine. "Female sexuality has always been conceptualized on the basis of masculine parameters,"[11] and women's pleasure is "denied by a civilization that privileges phallomorphism."[12] But sexual difference can, of course, be understood outside the binary, as an economy that paradoxically transcends it. To speak of binaries is to assume equilibrium, a balancing of two terms or values. To speak of difference already introduces disproportion, heterogeneity, the caesura of dualism. Moreover, Irigaray emphasizes plurality rather than the dyad, thereby allowing difference to disrupt that other infamous duality – clitoris and vagina.

"Body, breasts, pubis, clitoris, labia, vulva, vagina, neck of the uterus, womb, . . . and this *nothing* that already gives pleasure by setting them apart from each other,"[13] she writes. The multiple zones cannot be unified, remain spaced apart, which is why they privilege pleasure over the open–closed, passive–active pairings.

Yet how this caesura, too, has been condemned! Valerie Traub claims that it is still caught up in a strict equating of parts of the body and desire.

The psychomorphology of Irigaray's feminine body would then still be dependent on a "logic of . . . equivalence."[14] An equivalence between the lips and female desire. Meanwhile, for Traub, the logic of equivalence is "secured by the phallus."[15] Indeed, for Lacan, it is the phallus that enjoys the "power of naming" and assigning a meaningful value to a part of the body, thereby allowing it to become the emblem of erotic identity.

But, even at the supposed risk of a rigidifying identity, isn't trying to think and write female pleasure a necessary step? Isn't that still the case? It's not clear that Irigaray fell into the trap of a phallic symbolizing of the clitoris that would make it a primary value for women's bodies since, in her words, the clitoris "resists . . . a firm foundation."[16]

In proposing her geography of feminine pleasure, Irigaray sought to double, intensify and thereby transgress the Freudian vision (and Lacanian too, at another level) of women's genitals. To assert the existence of a sex "that is not one" is to refuse to reduce sex to a sexual organ, to divert the anatomical vocabulary from its originary anchoring so as to orient it toward the construction of an unimaginable body from the point of view of psychoanalysis. Is this type of excess, initiated by Beauvoir and radicalized by Irigaray, now of no use? Irigaray writes:

> But Freud needs this support from anatomy in order to justify a theoretical position, especially in his description of woman's sexual development . . . in the name of that anatomical destiny, women are seen as less favored by nature from the point of view of libido; they are often frigid, nonaggressive, nonsadistic, nonpossessive, homosexual depending upon the degree to which their ovaries are hermaphroditic, they are outsiders where cultural values are concerned unless they participate in them through some sort of "mixed heredity," and so on. In short, they are deprived of the worth of their sex. The important thing, of course, is that no one should know who has deprived them, or why, and that "nature" be held accountable.[17]

It had to happen. The Freudian anatomical diktat had to be undone, unmoored through the proposal of another bodily schema. Today, this schema is seen as revisable, plastic, not necessarily feminine, but it was Irigaray who laid the groundwork for this transformational rewriting of the body.

Another critique of Irigaray is that she writes only for lesbians. In *This Sex which Is Not One*, in the chapter "When Our Lips Speak Together," it is clear that the lips are the lips of (at least two) women in a loving embrace. She writes: "We are luminous. Neither one nor two. I've never known how to count. Up to you. In their calculations, we make two. Really, two? Doesn't that make you laugh? An odd sort of two. And yet not one. Especially not one. Let's leave *one* to them."[18]

Is this a problem? Aren't there several possible ways to interpret this scene? And anyhow, isn't it always true that, as Audre Lorde said, "the true feminist deals out of a lesbian consciousness whether or not she ever sleeps with women"?[19]

10

"With Tenderness and Respect for the Blameless Vulva"

In their 2018 report on "female sexual mutilation," French senators Maryvonne Blondin and Marta de Cidrac offered two necessary terminological clarifications to what are too rapidly called (I've made the mistake myself) excision and clitoridectomy.[1]

The first is the phrase itself, "mutilations sexuelles féminines" (MSF), or female sexual mutilation, which is now the official term in France. This appellation is the result of several formulations and reformulations undertaken since the late 1950s, which testify to evolving perceptions.

They explain: "In 1958 when the UN, and in 1959 the WHO, took up these issues for the first time, mutilations were understood as customary ritualistic procedures."[2] At that time, excision, for example, was equated with circumcision.

However, from the mid-1970s, these "procedures" were increasingly viewed as violence against women. Hence, the recognition in the official term "mutilation." While, in the United Kingdom, some prefer the notion of female genital cutting (FGC), and the phrase chosen by the WHO is female genital mutilation (FGM), Francophone countries prefer to refer to female *sexual* mutilation. In 2013, the Commission nationale consultative des droits de l'homme (CNCDH), the French national advisory commission on human rights, declared that

the notion of female sexual mutilation refers to the "violation of the fundamental rights of girls and women," thereby emphasizing that "these mutilations must be combatted, above all, on the ground of the rights of the human person" and must not "be reduced to medical issues" nor to the "biological aspect of the practice" as the term "genital mutilations" implies.[3]

The second clarification involves an acknowledgment of the range of different sexual mutilations, also signaling a significant evolution from the mid-1950s:

> The typology designated by the WHO in 1997, and revised in 2007, recognizes three principal types of mutilation, all of which affect external female genitalia for non-medical reasons:
>
> – Type 1 – Clitoridectomy: the partial or total removal of the clitoral glans and/or the clitoral hood;
> – Type 2 – Excision: the partial or total removal of the clitoral glans and the labia minora, with or without the removal of the labia majora;
> – Type 3 – Infibulation: the narrowing of the vaginal opening by cutting and repositioning the labia minora and/or labia majora, with or without the removal of the clitoral hood and glans. The resulting scar must be cut at the time of marriage and/or childbirth. This type of mutilation, which is less common, appears to occur largely in East Africa.
> – Type 4 – All the other harmful procedures

done to the female genitalia for non-medical purposes, e.g. pricking, piercing, incising, scraping and cauterizing the genital area.[4]

According to CNCDH, a girl or woman is excised in the world every 15 seconds. Among the 200 million victims counted today, 44 million are less than 15 years old. A report by the parliamentary assembly of the Council of Europe asserts that "any parallel between male circumcision and female genital mutilation must be rejected, if only because the clitoris, whose sole function is sexual pleasure, has no male equivalent."[5] For Doctor Emmanuelle Piet, President of the Collectif feministe contre le viol [feminist collective against rape], mutilations "seek to remove female pleasure: on these grounds, it is indeed a matter of sexual mutilation."[6]

"Halimata Fofana, author of *Mariama, l'écorchée vive*, remembers the searing pain of the repeated movements of the exciser's knife, the burning caused by disinfection with 90 percent alcohol on the raw wound, how it was impossible to either walk or to sit for several days after the 'procedure.'" [7]

Another testimony of these traumas is found in the work of African-American feminist writer Alice Walker, whose style and poetic creativity are so powerful. Walker's militant activism sits at the intersection of two battles – namely, Black civil rights, and the abolition of female genital mutilation. Written in 1992, *Possessing the Secret of Joy*,[8] is no doubt the first novel written on the issue of mutilations. It was followed in 1993 by a book and associated documentary with the same title, made by filmmaker Pratibha Parmar: *Warrior Marks: Female Genital Mutilation and the Sexual Blinding of Women.*[9] In this work, Walker travels to Africa to study excision. The film ends with an interview with an exciser – who is herself "mutilated" – as she prepares to undertake a "procedure."

The opening images of the film show a group of women singing: "We condemn FGM." One of them, midwife Comfort I. Ottah, turns toward the camera and says: "This is not culture, this is torture."[10] Or, as Elfriede Jelinek puts it,

Women's forced silence concerning what they endure is another wound, one inflicted when they open their mouths too wide. Because lust is not

79

for them in the same way speech is not, and above all, if they are talking about whatever is "never talked about." As long as woman the wound, the disabled, the one who is "missing something," is perceived by masters of the discourse and regrettably also by accomplices as the (already) mutilated one, nothing will change.[11]

The mutilations are abysses of pain that become twisted badges of power – the power of those who do not believe in the pain.

"I did not realize for a long time that I was dead."[12] These are the opening words of *Possessing the Secret of Joy*, spoken by Tashi, born in Africa but who lives in the United States since her marriage to Adam. Loyalty to her ancestral culture – the culture of the (fictional) Olinkas society – prompted Tashi, already Americanized through her relationship with Adam, the son of a missionary, to subject herself voluntarily in adolescence to the knife of the *tsunga* (exciser). She saw it as a means to demonstrate her loyalty to her people. But the excision was a terrible trauma, condemning the young woman to spend her whole life battling madness and trying in vain to understand the ancestral reasons for these mutilations.

In the end, through psychoanalysis, she managed to find a type of bodily wholeness, as she explains: "just at the end of my life, I am beginning to reinhabit completely the body I long ago left."[13] Tashi experiences another psychic blow when she remembers the scene of her older sister Dura's excision, which led to her hemorrhaging to death. She recalls the particularly painful memory of M'Lissa, the exciser, throwing Dura's genitalia to a hungry hen who, "as if waiting for this moment, rushed toward M'Lissa's upturned foot, located the flung object in the air and then on the ground, and in one quick movement of beak and neck, gobbled it down."[14] For Tashi, the excision is an assassination. She eventually returns to Africa to take revenge by stabbing the exciser to death – blade against blade – before she is condemned to death herself.

Three threads are interwoven in the story: a condemnation of genital mutilations, women's forced complicity with patriarchal power and the need to break the silence. As a chorus, we hear the voices of Audre Lorde – "Your silence will not protect you";[15] Toni Morrison with her "rememory" in *Beloved*[16] (echoing Tashi's words: "If you lie to yourself about your own pain, you will be killed by those who will claim you enjoyed it"[17]); and bell hooks: "many black women are struggling to accept and love our bodies. For some of us that means learning to love our skin color. Others of us may love our blackness but mentally mutilate, cutting the body into desirable and undesirable parts . . . Loving our flesh, celebrating it, includes the eroticism of language, the way we talk to one another";[18] "Since so many black women have experienced traumatic physical abuse; we come to sexuality wounded."[19]

For Walker, as for so many who echo her words, the mutilations of women in Africa are no different from the physical violence, sexual abuse and rape that Black women in the United States suffer, and that all point to the heritage of slavery. Like slavery, genital mutilations are a symbolic murder.

Victim or survivor? The right term is still up for discussion.

Mutilation and Repair:
In Search of *le mot juste*

There are ever more voices speaking out to con-
test the use of the term "mutilation." Whether
termed genital or sexual makes no difference, it
is argued, to the inappropriateness of the word.
Members of the LGBT community, researchers
and doctors are now all questioning the relevance
of this standard phraseology, officially recognized by the WHO, which is a major actor in the
debate. As we have seen, the descriptor sexual (or
genital) mutilation implies that any intervention
on female genitalia without a medical reason is a
case of torture, a violation of the right to bodily
integrity and is not primarily a matter of cultural
practices. The descriptors MSF and FGM would
thus constitute, in and of themselves, forms of

discrimination.[1] It is noted, moreover, that the WHO considers only non-Western forms of these procedures.

Why should female mutilations be symptomatized and singled out while other interventions are made without consent on intersex children (operations or hormonal treatments) and on all those who are affected by variations in sexual development,[2] for example? And why exclude circumcision?

In a searing article, "Current Critiques of the WHO Policy on Female Genital Mutilation," researchers Brian D. Earp and Sara Johnsdotter show why anti-FGM laws may be both ethically and legally questionable.[3] They explain:

> The appropriateness of applying the term "mutilation" to all of these procedures as such (that is, without regard to their severity, their typical or likely consequences, the means by which they are carried out, the context in which they occur, the reasons for which they are done – apart from ill-defined "medical reasons" – or even the capacity of the affected person to consent), has been questioned on several grounds.[4]

To start with, the term "mutilation" is very vague. It includes a wide range of interventions that do not have the same consequences for sexuality and health. For example, "procedures, such as ritual nicking or pricking, do not remove tissue, may cause no lasting functional impairments, and often result in no visible change to the morphology of the external female genitalia."[5]

Secondly, the term "mutilation" discredits the motives of those who practice or authorize the procedures:

> it implies an intent to harm or disfigure: parents of all cultural backgrounds who request a genital cutting procedure for their child – female, male, or intersex/DSD – virtually never take themselves to be causing net bodily harm or disfigurement; rather, the typical aim is to improve or enhance the child's body in line with locally-prevailing socio-medical, religious, aesthetic, or (other) cultural norms.[6]

Let us recall that, according to current medical norms, a body is considered genetically male with a chromosome combination XY, and genetically female with a chromosome combination XX.

Children who are "intersex" (this term is strongly criticized) undergo procedures transforming their genitals up to the moment of pre-adolescence. If, after chromosomal analysis, the intersex newborn is considered genetically female (XX), for example, surgical interventions remove the genital tissue that might be taken for a penis. The reconstruction of the vulva (along with the reduction of the clitoris) generally begins around the age of three months. If the visible organ resembles what medical terminology terms a penis-clitoris, the procedure usually involves a transformation of the clitoris into a penis.

But what degree of indeterminacy might be considered standard to authorize intervention on the genitalia of a child?

Another argument proposed against the use of the word "mutilation" relates to the fact that it is never used to refer to Western forms of mutilation that are equally invasive: "for example, 'cosmetic' labiaplasty – increasingly performed on young adolescent girls in the US, UK, and elsewhere."[7]

Moreover, "the language of 'mutilation' is

applied indiscriminately to all non-Western forms of medically unnecessary genital cutting affecting females . . . while no form of medically unnecessary . . . male genital cutting (MGC) is officially described as 'mutilation,' no matter how severe, degrading, involuntary, unhygienic, risky, disabling, or disfiguring."[8]

So why not invert the equation between excision and circumcision (female) to instead view circumcision as a form of excision (male)?[9] Circumcision also involves risks of infection, herpes and neurological problems when done with instruments that are not sterilized, without anesthetic – to say nothing of its negative consequences on sex life. So why, then, was the equating of circumcision and excision, which was accepted in the 1950s, subsequently prohibited in France? Is the ban really justifiable?

One more point: the term "mutilation" may affect pleasure on its own count. It can, in fact, needlessly stigmatize women, causing negative consequences for self-image and self-esteem, thereby increasing the risk of aggravating the trauma. Many consider the term defamatory. Young women who are described as "excised," "without a clitoris," in a Western country (these terms are themselves Western) may develop a complex, thinking that they will always be excluded from sexual pleasure and orgasm, while "that is not necessarily the case."[10]

What is it that erases pleasure then? The act of mutilation, or the word itself?

Mutilation erases pleasure: can the two possible meanings of this statement co-exist in the narrow caesura that separates them? Is there a distance between language and itself, between a statement and itself? How can we (avoid) hearing simultaneously the condemnation of FSM or FGM and the rejection of the very terms of this condemnation?

As Delphine Gardey puts it:

How can we bring together the correctness or justice of the arguments? Must we be myopic or inhuman in the name of respecting difference and the battle against neo-colonialism? Can't we mobilize when we see serious attacks on other people? Can one be an "activist" without disrespecting or criticizing other cultures? And are there any alternatives to these dead-ends? Does criticizing "female sexual mutilation" mean imposing dominant Western norms? Does not doing so amount

to endorsing practices such as excision or support-
ing their continuation?[11]

Does contemporary feminism present, or present itself, as a form of schizophrenia?

12

Technologically Modified Bodies:
Paul B. Preciado and Transfeminism

At this point you attempt to wrench out m/y
kidneys. They resist you. You touch m/y green gall-
bladder. *I* have a deathly chill, *I* moan, *I* fall into
an abyss, m/y head is awhirl, m/y heart is in m/y
mouth, it feels as if m/y blood is all congealed in
m/y arteries.

> (Monique Wittig, *The Lesbian Body*, trans.
> David Le Vay, Boston: Beacon Press,
> 1986, p. 38)

There's no such thing as an intact body – a body
that is naturally what it is and whose gender
identity has experienced no transformations
whatsoever. Perhaps the line between transformation and mutilation is a fine one. These questions

are at the heart of the work of transfeminist philosopher Paul B. Preciado. Starting with the intimate imbrication of biology and technology, from *Counter-Sexual Manifesto*[1] to *Testo Junkie*,[2] then from *An Apartment on Uranus*[3] to the recent *Can the Monster Speak?*,[4] Preciado has described and analyzed the metamorphoses of his body and gender, his psychic mutations, the plastic constitution of his identity, which, from Beatriz, who they were to start with, led her to become him, Paul. Preciado writes:

I became queer when the AIDS crisis started to kill the best of all of us. I moved into the transgender movement when hormones became a political code. I have been slowly transitioning for the last eight years, using testosterone in gel in low doses to modulate my female-to-male gender. But during the last six months, I've decided to jump to a different speed. I am injecting myself with testosterone every 10 days. I have also changed my name to Paul. Hair is growing on my legs. Meanwhile, my face is becoming Paul's face. Political subjectivity is being fabricated between language and biochemical molecules.[5]

In 2017, Preciado became a "man" in the eyes of the law, but they do not recognize themself subjectively as either man or woman, claiming "non-binary" instead.

In this work, life and body that are constantly reinventing themselves, all dichotomies are blown to pieces, including the distinction between cis and trans subjects. The term "zissexuell,"[6] today more often referred to as cisgender, appeared in the early 2000s to describe "individuals whose birth gender, body and personal identity coincide." Thus, a "cisgender" man or woman is someone whose assigned sex at birth and social gender are aligned. More capacious than the category "transsexual," the descriptor "transgender" refers to individuals whose gender identity differs from the sex assigned at birth. In Latin, *cis* means "from the same side" while *trans* means "from the other side." Classics scholars might recall that, since the time of Gaul, cisalpine has meant "on this side of the Alps" and transalpine "beyond the Alps."[7]

There are, in fact, not two, but rather a multiplicity of sides, inclinations, profiles and frontiers. A multiplicity of genders and even clitorises. You never do have your gender. Rather, gender has the subject, putting them into motion like a machine. This machine is a network of logistical, biomedical and cultural norms that systematically disrupt the heterosexual order. What woman has never transformed her body by taking estrogen or progesterone? Isn't a cis woman's body always already trans from ingesting hormones in the Pill or from replacement therapy during menopause, to mention just two common examples? Consequently, the subject of transfeminism is not women or men but rather "users of technologies such as the pill, Viagra, testosterone, Prozac, Truvada. . . ."[8] Today,

> this is a somatopolitical revolution: the uprising of all vulnerable bodies against technologies of oppression. Inspired by Haraway's manifesto, neither man nor woman but the mutant hacker is a key figure in transfeminism. The question is not: What am I? What gender or what sexuality? But rather: How does it work? How can we interfere in its functioning? And, more importantly: How could it work in another way?[9]

I repeat: there is no body unscathed, no body untouched by pharmacological artefacts and prostheses. In this sense, all bodies – not just women's bodies – are fragile because they are manufactured. Mutilated.

Although he calls out the effects of biopolitics, Preciado does not, for all that, hate biology. In his view, the constructed aspect of gender never erases the materiality, the empiricism of the sanguine, glandular, epigenetics of sex. This materiality is part and parcel of the genesis of gender. In what does a body's matter consist? Judith Butler already asked this question in *Bodies that Matter*.[10] For Preciado, gender is implicated in the carnal order of sex, blood, entrails and organs. And this is precisely why gender is not simply performative: "it is entirely constructed, and, at the same time, it is purely organic . . . Their carnal plasticity destabilizes the distinction between the imitated and the imitator, between the truth and the representation of the truth, between the reference and the referent, between nature and artifice, between sexual organs and sexual practices."[11]

Sex is precisely the interchange that enables traffic between the symbolic and material dimensions of the body. On the one hand, "it defines sex as technology."[12] On the other, it does not exist without "particular organs" and "particular anatomical reactions."[13] Gender manufactures sex; yet, sex influences gender, sending it chemical signals, transmitting impulses. Thus, the sensitive tissue of the body never disappears. Referring to his new "masculine" voice, Preciado declares: "It is with this voice, fabricated yet organic, staged yet entirely my own, that I address you today, esteemed ladies and gentlemen of the Academy."[14]

Who exactly are these "ladies and gentlemen of the Academy"? *Can the Monster Speak?* is the text of a lecture given in 2019 to 3,500 French psychoanalysts gathered at the Palais des congrès in Paris to discuss the theme of women and psychoanalysis. Apparently, the battle for transfeminism was news to them. Preciado recounts:

The speech triggered an earthquake. When I asked whether there was a psychoanalyst in the auditorium who was queer, trans or non-binary, there was silence, broken only by giggles. When I asked that psychoanalytic institutions face up to their responsibilities in response to contemporary discursive changes in the epistemology of sexual and gender identity, half the audience laughed and the other half shouted or demanded that I leave the premises.[15]

Other members of the audience brought up the supposedly irreducible nature of sexual difference. Preciado responds:

Don't tell me that sex, gender and sexual difference is not crucial in explaining the structure of the psychic apparatus in psychoanalysis. The entire Freudian edifice is conceived from the position of patriarchal masculinity, from the heterosexual male body seen as a body with an erect penis, penetrating and ejaculating; this is why "women" in psychoanalysis, those strange creatures (sometimes) equipped with a reproductive uterus and clitoris, remain and will remain a problem. This is why, in 2019, you still feel the need to set aside a day to talk about "women in psychoanalysis."[16]

Here we are – we've come full circle! Fifty years to circumnavigate the globe, psyche and bodies. From Dolto's talk at the Congress on Feminine Sexuality to Preciado's talk on transgender at the Congress on Women and Psychoanalysis, everything has changed – or maybe nothing has.

13

Nymphs 4
Nymphomaniac

"Mea vulva, mea maxima vulva"

Lars von Trier's film *Nymphomaniac* was not well received.[1] Considered shocking, unnecessarily provocative and gory, it had to be sanitized, and the version available today is not the original. The film has two parts, *Nymphomaniac* I and *Nymphomaniac* II. The main character, a woman named Joe (a tribute to Jimi Hendrix's song, "Hey Joe"), recounts her story in several "chapters" to a man called Seligman. The entire film is a flashback of their conversations.

Joe begins life with a close relationship to her father, a botanist. After asking her neighbor, Jerôme, to take her virginity, the young Joe soon discovers she is a nymphomaniac. Enjoying several lovers, usually at the same time (I wish

I could spend time on the scene in which the woman who has been cheated on, played by Uma Thurman, arrives with her two sons to demonize her husband who left her for an entirely impassive Joe), she runs into Jerôme several years later and marries him. The early days of the marriage are happy, with a perfect sexual harmony. But, all of a sudden, Joe's pleasure stops: "I can't feel anything anymore," she says, and, explaining to Seligman, "In a single moment I lost all sexual feeling, my cunt simply went numb."

She and Jerôme have a child, Marcel, whom Joe rejects immediately after a caesarian birth that disgusts her. In a bid to rediscover her pleasure, with Jerôme's consent, she returns to multiple erotic encounters with strangers (hence the scene with two Black men that was considered so shocking). But she only finds ecstasy again with one anonymous man, a strange professional paid by women to hit them and who refuses any sexual exchange with them other than the beating. He gives nicknames to his clients but never knows their true identity: Joe is "Fido." We see her, crouched over the arm of a sofa, bound, head down, having the only bare part of her body, the flesh of her buttocks, thrashed with a whip and knotted rope. Pleasure returns, intensely. Her relationship with Jerôme doesn't last. The couple separate; Marcel is taken in by child welfare.

Joe now has to work to earn a living, but the head of the office requires her to go to therapy since her sexual obsession (she continues to pursue multiple experiences, this time with her coworkers) becomes incompatible with her employment. She starts to attend group sessions, organized along the model of Alcoholics Anonymous, in which each "patient" (strangely, there are only women in the group) must always begin by saying "I have an addiction to this or that." Joe must follow the rule by announcing "I am a sex addict." She would have preferred to say: "I am a nymphomaniac," but the therapist prohibits her from doing so. The difference between sex addict and nymphomaniac is not explained, it is simply imposed on her. Is it more correct to say *sex addict*? This new concept of sex addiction calls for close analysis. What does it add? What does it detract from nymphomania? Can one really be *addicted* to sex as to heroin? Whatever the case, like Joe, I find the expression absurd.

At first, Joe submits to the rule of this new, politically correct terminology, but soon she revolts against the therapist and leaves the group, shouting out her scorn for the other members and asserting herself now again as a nymphomaniac.

Later, Joe is contacted by a mafia organization which, knowing her S&M talents and supposed moral depravity, employ her to forcefully collect debts. Accompanied by two henchmen, her task is to get debtors to admit their most secret fantasies, and torment them at once physically and psychologically. Her "boss" then asks her to investigate an adolescent girl, P, to try her out to see whether she would be suitable for the same line of work. Joe goes on to have an erotic relationship with the young girl.

It happens that Jerôme is one of the mafia "company" debtors. P is chosen to make him admit and pay up, but she falls in love with him and they have a relationship, causing Joe to despair.

Joe, who claims that she never felt love for anyone other than her father, realizes that in fact she is in love with both Jerôme and P and cannot help but feel jealous. One evening, she watches for the lovers in an underground passageway and tries to kill Jerôme, but the gun jams. Jerôme beats her brutally, has sex with P in front of her and then leaves her lying on the ground. Before leaving the spot, P urinates on Joe. This time the nymph does indeed *piss*.

Joe is rescued by Seligman who, while also walking through the passageway, sees her and picks her up. Joe tells him her story, which Seligman punctuates with commentaries, connecting each of Joe's tales to key moments in Western culture, music, painting, mathematics . . . as well as fishing and hunting traditions.

Joe tells him she has decided to be done with her past – which, for her, now implies total sexual abstinence. Seligman listens to her with great benevolence. However, unexpectedly, and in a terribly disappointing scene, he tries to penetrate her while she is sleeping. This time the gun does not jam.

The film is of a rare intensity, and it seems to me that it was misunderstood by those who vehemently vilified it. Disturbing and magnificent – Charlotte Gainsbourg offers a strikingly realistic portrait – the film is both raw and true. As always with von Trier, the power of its truth is simultaneously unbearable and undeniable.

It is important to recount the story in detail because it does not fit any existing narrative.

The full intensity of the film concentrates in the caesura between the raw, unexplained fact of a sexuality lived as hell and the course of a woman's life. This is why Joe's itinerary is not only narrative but – and more importantly – morphological. Far from the ordinary "The Sexual Life of . . .," *Nymphomaniac* shows the forming of a body in sharp dissonance with its sexuality, from early childhood to the adult years. For five Joes, there are five actresses: Ronja Rissman is Joe at age 2; Maja Arsovic, Joe at 7; Ananya Berg, Joe at 10; Stacy Martin, from ages 15 to 30; Charlotte Gainsbourg, from 30 to 40. Five Joes who dissolve into one another, reminding each of the other in vertiginous echoes.

The morphology of sexual dissonance lies in the mystery of the sudden disappearance of pleasure. A pleasure that must now be sought at a distance, far off in a violence beyond sadomasochism. So far, in fact, that the quest attains a sort of paradoxical saintliness. In this absolute search for the absolute, Seligman's character appears as a nod to God. The disappeared pleasure materializes in a wound: the wound of the clitoris.

Over the course of four hours, we see the clitoris only once, in an anatomical representation. Is it even a clitoris, or the cleft of the labia? Hard to say. Several close-ups linger over Joe's buttocks and she is seen from behind, bound by her torturer. There is one, single cunnilingus, also filmed close-up. But the only real, visible stage appearance of the clitoris is as a wound. One day in the bathroom, Joe discovers that her clitoris is bleeding: "My clitoris started to bleed more and more often." So when P wants to make love with her for the first time, Joe resists: "I have a wound."

Why is it bleeding? How would sexual abuse cause this? Is it from the whip? Given its position, that's unlikely. It seems rather that it is a symbolic wound. The dead zone of compulsion. As if the clitoris were untouchable. Sanctified and damned. The victim of a devouring vagina that is never full enough – in a restaurant, on Jerôme's request, Joe fills it with a dozen dessert spoons – the clitoris is bathed in the blood of its mystery.

What is genius in the film is linking nymphomania to the absence of pleasure and to the wound. Sexuality is the experience of physical, social, moral and psychic violence. Solitude, atomization, abandon, detachment, separation. Only violence produces an orgasm.

Seligman compares Joe to the nymph used in fly fishing. The nymph is bait made with a ball and piece of lead wire trimmed with either horsehair or hair wrapped around the hook. As a young girl, Joe is the nymph, the beautiful mermaid who doesn't know that in the midst of her body a little harpoon hides in place of her clitoris.

In *Nymphomaniac*, the nymph is neither muse, ideal nor image but, instead, the distress of a body bearing the death of pleasure. Lars von Trier has been criticized for privileging sex to the detriment of gender. I don't think this critique is fair (Joe is, after all, a non-binary name). As in all of his films, he stops at the edge of difference between woman and the feminine, a wounded difference, whose organ is only ever seen as a negative or transparency.

My reservation is about opting for permanent abstinence as a solution to the tortures of pleasure. But perhaps von Trier thinks that the only solution to erased pleasure is further erasure.

14

Ecstasy Zones in the Real

Womanism is to Feminism what Purple is to Lavender.

(Alice Walker, *In Search of Our Mothers' Gardens: Womanist Prose*, London: Hachette UK, 1983)

In *Changing Difference: The Feminine and the Question of Philosophy*,[1] I recounted my experience as a woman philosopher, analyzing my own intellectual itinerary and textual practice.

What I wanted to communicate was the effect that entering into a powerful discipline of the mind (philosophy is just one such example) can have on the sexuality and gender of the person – be they he or she – who joins such a circle of thought. I believed, and still do, that beyond its singularity – or rather precisely because of it – my experience might be edifying. The time had come to abandon the belief that philosophizing and "de-gendering" go hand in hand. Along with Irigaray, I had come to accept that "speech is never neutral."[2] I had to stop hiding behind the supposed asexuality of the philosophical subject – the argument usually forwarded by women in order to survive in the concentrate of categorical testosterone that is traditional philosophical discourse.

I'll admit that today I'm far less interested in tracking down textual phallocentrism than in exploring the somatic shaping power of philosophy. Contrary to what is generally assumed, philosophy shapes bodies. I tried to show this elsewhere in regard to the relation between thought and its other organ – the brain. Philosophy does not do work on bodies solely for orthopedic purposes. It's not just about disciplining. It also sculpts an erotics that enables new connections between intellectual energy and libidinal energy. I am not referring to an idealized or metaphorical sexuality; I'm talking about a sexualizing effect of discourse.

Coming into philosophy and coming into my body eventually melded together to become one and the same experience. Clearly, I no longer have the same body since I think, so to speak. Rather, I now have several bodies, such that I should say, "coming into philosophy and coming into my *bodies* eventually melded together." My efforts to loosen up my desire, to enrich my "sexual relationships" with other partners – he, she, they are not only real, but also virtual, logical, textual – also shaped my clitoris, left it trembling, quivering, alive in an entirely new way that has nothing to do with sublimation.

It's not about my non-binary mind and my clitoridian body. Intellectual non-binarism is the opposite of a de-sexualization. Likewise, the clitoridian libido is not separate from the intellect. My clitoris is on synchronous alert with my brain; the burning line stretches from one extremity of my being to the other. Strangely, this line challenges me to "identify" myself sexually, even as the categories available for doing so become increasingly porous.

Before, according to the fairly conventional norms that I repeatedly failed to meet, I was a girl. For me, philosophy was – and still is – the success of this failure. It taught me to doubt my femininity, enabling the multiplication of my genders – that is, philosophy gave me yet another reason to doubt my femininity. My clitoris already had a double life, as sex and gender, as anatomical and social existence. Philosophy added a political life as a transgender clitoris.

It seems to me that "feminine" is the least inadequate word to describe this situation. A feminine outside sexual difference, outside heteronormativity. A feminine of *subjectification*. I do not share critiques of the word "feminism," which, unlike transfeminism, is suspected of being more attached to identity politics than to a process of disidentification. Jacques Rancière is correct when he writes that "any subjectification is a disidentification, removal from the naturalness of a place, the opening up of a subject space where anyone can be counted since it is the space where those of no account are counted."[3] Thus, "in politics 'woman' is the subject of experience – the denatured, defeminized subject – that measures the gap between an acknowledged part . . . and a having no part."[4]

I know it is difficult both to hear and to make this argument heard, but, let me repeat, woman and feminine are not exactly one and the same. It is this excess of the feminine in relation to woman, this plasticity of gender in relation to gender, that the clitoris brings to our attention. The complicity of the clitoris with the feminine derives from the fact that both survive their erasures, their mutilations, all the violence to which they are subjected. Like indestructible revenants. Marking a space that is empty, but open.

I believe that, around this space, feminisms can listen to each other even if they do not agree. I'll give three examples of these different feminisms.

Radical Italian feminist Silvia Federici, author of the well-known *Caliban and the Witch: Women, the Body and Primitive Accumulation*,[5] was fiercely criticized because, in her recent *Beyond the Periphery of the Skin*,[6] she accused both gender theory and transfeminism of masking the question of the feminine. While I do not defend her position, I understand her frustration and suffering. Pointing to all the violence done to women in the world, she argues "if 'women' is discarded as an analytic/political category, then 'feminism' must follow suit."[7] This statement, with its tendency to universalize an experience of oppression, is certainly debatable.[8] But, as Mara

Mantanaro emphasizes in her fine review of the book, Federici's claim is, in fact, more about the feminine than about woman. As Mantanaro writes: "women's bodies are . . . a field of inter-sections of material and symbolic forces and there is no anatomical destiny. The goal of the feminist protest movement was all about . . . *denaturalizing* femininity, that is, denaturalizing what a woman should be and do."[9] To repeat, then, the feminine can be defined as that which comes after woman is denaturalized. Its haunting remains, irreducible, and the violence of acts that seek to erase it immediately transform it into a phantom limb. Like a clitoris cut. That's why its negation hurts. I share Federici's doubts about a feminism excised from the feminine.

The weakness of Federici's argument lies in thinking that gender theory and transfeminism are not concerned about these doubts, that they sweep away the ghostly persistence of the feminine in a single stroke.

Turning to a second voice, in *Can the Monster Speak?*, Preciado writes: "I decided to stop being a woman. Why couldn't abandoning femininity not become a fundamental tactic of feminism?"[10] This statement appears to be the opposite of what

Federici says. But Preciado is referring to woman here, not the feminine. To dismiss and to mourn are not the same thing. Paul abandons femininity, but perhaps not the feminine, since all his books bear her mourning. As he says:

> contrary to what medicine and psychiatry believe and promulgate, I have not completely ceased to be Beatriz to become solely Paul. My living body, I will not say my unconscious or my consciousness, but my living body, which encompasses all its constant mutation and its multiple evolutions, is like a Greek city in which, at varying levels of energy, contemporary trans buildings, postmodern lesbian architecture and beautiful Art Deco houses coexist with ancient rustic buildings beneath whose foundations lie classical ruins both animal and vegetal, mineral and chemical substrates that tend to be invisible. The traces of past life left in my memory have become more and more complex and interconnected, creating a collection of living forces.[11]

What survives is always alive. Evidently, the feminine is a full bookshelf in this library of the body . . .

A third striking line of thinking on this difficult relation to the feminine comes from American transgender theorist and academic Jack Halberstam, who analyzes the resentment felt by some lesbians in regard to transgender FTMs (Female-to-Male), whom they see as "betraying" the feminine by no longer being women: "Some lesbians seem to see FTMs as traitors to a 'woman's' movement who cross over and become the enemy. Some FTMs see lesbian feminism as a discourse that has demonized them and their masculinity. Some butches consider FTMs to be butches who 'believe in anatomy,' and some FTMs consider butches to be FTMs who are too afraid to transition."[12]

This incisive article shows that "abandoning" a gender is a fraught question in non-heterosexual contexts as well, even causing a border war between queer and transgender. Halberstam recounts how he had asked the following naive question in an earlier text: "why, in this age of gender transitivity, when we have agreed that gender is a social construct, is transsexuality a wide-scale phenomenon?"[13] Does transsexuality imply a sort of anatomical reclaiming? A renaturalizing of gender via sex? Halberstam goes on to state: "I was also implicitly examining the possibility of the nonoperated-upon transgender-identified person."[14] This reflection is particularly interesting since Halberstam has the courage to ask what exactly is given up in the event of a surgical transition. What disappears and what remains of the feminine?[15]

It might be argued that the same issues arise in regard to the "masculine." But that's not entirely true. There's no question that masculinity doesn't necessarily coincide with virility or with the anatomical fact of being a man. But so many studies, analyses, representations – artistic or other – have been devoted to this anatomy, this virility, to the logics of masculinity in general, that we simply cannot equate them with approaches to feminine anatomy, where the representations and schema amount to no more than a few stereotyped snapshots. Clearly, there is a disproportionate visibility here. Hence the need to always bring back the ghost – that is, the reality of the feminine.

But what meaning can a philosopher's experience have for non-philosophers? It's just the same as any confession – any narrative of initiation, trauma or transition. Throughout this story, "I" am no more myself than any other person, be they he or she. No one has the choice. The biological body is never alone or self-sufficient. It always moves beyond its first casing (Beauvoir speaks of "transcendence"), shaped by discourses, norms, representations. A body is always an arrangement for the transfer, circulation and telepathy between an anatomical reality and a symbolic projection. If the body were nothing but an anatomical given, it would not survive its wounds. It must always remain in the world and this labor of accommodation assumes a departure from the self, the setting up of a hub between the biological and symbolic, body and flesh of the world. The symbolic is not the tomb of matter; it is its relocation. Philosophy is my personal hub. Just one example of re-identifying disidentification. But there are others – so many others.

For me, the only way to survive the phallocentrism of philosophy is to assert that philosophy is non-binary – which, I repeat, is not to make it neutral. This non-binarism signals that it can be deconstructed. The deconstruction of a conceptual or systematic edifice must include what Derrida termed a "*defective* cornerstone."[16] In fact, this "stone" marks the presence of another sex, another gender of texts, which alone makes these texts legible. A clitoridian zone of the *logos*.

The clitoris in texts signals the place where philosophers pleasure themselves and give up identifying with their anatomical sex and social gender. This place is not always immediately visible. Official canons of interpretation obviously try to rub it out. They fail. In the caesura between texts and themselves, there settle in an entire series of forms that shake up the framework of Western *logos* so as to open it always a little more to foreign bodies and unrecognized forms of orgasmic pleasure.

This is not philosophical essentialism. Again, there are countless hubs linking the biological and symbolic. The entire Real is ready to receive the symbolic projection of bodies, dappled as it is with clitoridian zones, zones of ecstasy that might resemble the Freudian erogenous zones, had this concept been a success.

So what do the ecstasy zones in the Real say?

This question allows me to express my discomfort with regard to some reclamations of the clitoris that are still too phallic for my liking. The title of one issue of the journal *Point[s] d'accroche* was "How to become a subject and assert oneself between the powerful penis and erectile clitoris."[17] In their commentary, the conveners mention that all too often the clitoris is equated with power, and ask therefore:

> Does the becoming subject necessarily imply "power" in the manner proclaimed by the logic of virile domination? Is masculinity the only model to follow to assert oneself as social subject? Is the only "pleasure" powerful, dominant, erectile . . .? Can't the clitoris be represented outside . . . a power relation (on *Sur les docks* [on the docks], Typhaine D calls the clitoris even more "powerful" than the penis since it is the only organ in the human body that is exclusively dedicated to pleasure, endowed as it is with the most nerve endings)?[18]

Preciado himself does not entirely avoid a certain discourse of power and success. When I was reading *An Apartment on Uranus*, I was surprised to come across the following metaphor:

> We are driving along San Francisco Bay in a car, by the Pacific Ocean. Annie Sprinkle is in the driver's

seat and I am co-pilot, along with her dog, Butch. . . . Annie Sprinkle tells me that San Francisco is the "clitoris of America," the tiniest and most powerful organ in the country: 121 ultra-electrified kilometers from which the silicon networks that connect the world emanate. Once there was gold fever, now it's cybernetic fever. Sex and technology. Sun and dollars. Activism and neoliberalism. Innovation and control. Google, Adobe, Cisco, eBay, Facebook, Tesla, Twitter . . . 121 square kilometers that concentrate one-third of the risk-capital of the United States.[19]

I can hardly see what distinguishes this vision of the superpower clitoris from the classic image of the erect phallus.

This "clitoris of America" is reminiscent of the famous distinction Roland Barthes draws between the *studium* and the *punctum* of a photograph: "the *studium* gives me the subject of the photo, leads me to 'encounter the photographer's intentions,' to enter into harmony with them, to approve or disapprove of them, but always to understand them."[20] The *studium* prompts a "sort of vague, slippery . . . interest."[21] Then, all of a sudden, something will break (or punctuate) the *studium*. This time it is not I who seek it out . . . it is this element which rises from the scene, shoots out of it like an arrow, and pierces me . . . I shall therefore call *punctum* . . . A photograph's *punctum* is that accident which pricks me (but also bruises me, is poignant to me).[22]

Defined as a concentration of power, the "clitoris of America" is like a *punctum*. If the body of America is a *studium*, the California-clitoris is the arrow that pierces it, stabs it, crosses the great space of the territory's "*average* affect"[23] of only mediocre interest.

For me, thinking the clitoris – or, rather, letting it think – implies escaping the *studium–punctum* duality, which leads back to the passive/active dichotomy and its disastrous effects, in terms both of the connotations of a logic of virility and of the renewal of the vaginal and the clitoridian that it revives.

Clitoridian pleasure is not the effect of piercing, penetration or stabbing. This also means that if the ecstasy zones in the Real are equally well zones where meaning is produced, this meaning shows without erupting – in every sense of the term.

Pleasure sits between *studium* and *punctum*, in their caesura; it is neither one nor the other. The clitoris – like the feminine – *relates to power* but is not a *power relation*. In any case, that's how mine thinks.

The clitoris is an anarchist.

15

Clitoris, Anarchy and the Feminine

In Greek, *an-arkhia* refers literally to the absence of first principle (*arkhê*) – that is, to a lack of command. Without command also means without beginning. *Arkhé* assigns a temporal order by privileging what comes first, both in the order of power and chronologically. Hence, anarchy means without hierarchy or origin. Anarchy calls into question dependence and derivation.

For centuries, the word "anarchy" signified nothing but disorder and chaos. Aristotle defined it as an army without a strategy. An army that suddenly scatters, no longer knowing whether it is coming or going. The soldiers look behind and, when they no longer see their general, see nothing but a void.

In the mid nineteenth century, anarchists turned these negative connotations upside down by claiming that "anarchy is order without power."[1] Soldiers without leaders must learn to organize themselves alone. Order without command or origin is not necessarily disorder – in fact, not at all – rather, it is an other arrangement, an order composed without domination. One that comes only of itself and that counts only on itself. An ordering arrangement without orders given.

The complicity between clitoris and anarchy derives first from their common lot as undocumented travelers – their secret, hidden, unfamiliar existence. Long has the clitoris been considered, it too, a troublemaker, one organ too many, pointless – mocking anatomical, political and social order through its libertarian independence, its pleasure dynamic detached from any principle or goal. There's no governing a clitoris. Despite all attempts to master it via patriarchal authority, psychoanalytic diktat, moral imperatives, the weight of custom or ancestral ballast – it resists. It resists domination because it is indifferent to power and potency.

Potency is nothing without actuality, without performance, as seen in the application of a law, an edict, a decree or even a piece of advice. Its power always awaits actualization. Acts, principles, laws and decrees in turn depend on the docility and good will of their subordinates. Together, action and authority weave the inextricable cloth of subordination. Meanwhile, the clitoris is neither authoritative nor acting. Nor is it the immature potential awaiting vaginal realization. It does not bend to the model of erection and flaccidity. The clitoris interrupts the logic of command and obedience. It does not lead. And that's exactly why it's disturbing.

Emancipation requires finding the tipping point at which power and domination subvert one another. Self-subversion is one of the key notions of anarchist thought. Domination cannot be overthrown solely from the outside. It has its own internal fault line, announcing its eventual ruin. Any instance that shows indifference to the pairing of action and authority exasperates systems of domination, revealing its internal fractures. The clitoris enters into the very core of potency, with its normative, ideological power, only to reveal the breakdown that permanently threatens it.

I see clitoris, anarchy and feminine as indissolubly linked. They form a resistance front aware of the authoritarian tendencies of resistance itself. The defeat of domination is one of the greatest challenges of our time. Clearly, feminism is one of the most active figures in these stakes – a highly exposed spearhead since, as I said, it is without *arkhé*.

But to be without a ruling order is not to be without memory. That is why it's essential we not amputate feminism from the feminine. The feminine is, first and foremost, a reminder; it recalls the multiple forms of violence done to women, yesterday and today – every instance of mutilation, rape, harassment, femicide. Clearly, the clitoris is in many ways the depositary of this memory, simultaneously symbolizing and incarnating all that is unbearable in the autonomy of women's pleasure. At the same time, as I have said, the feminine transcends woman, denaturalizes woman and, in so doing – beyond the depravity of all the terrible and tiny abusers – it envisages a political sphere that is an indifference to mastery.

The feminine is that which ties this memory to this future.

Notes

1 Erasures

1 In France, not until 2019 did the "five high school textbooks begin to represent the full anatomy of the clitoris": Marlène Thomas, *Libération*, Oct. 4, 2019. (Translator's note: unless otherwise stated, all translations from original texts are by Carolyn Shread.)

2 Carolyn Gersh, *Naming the Body: A Translation with Commentary and Interpretive Essays of Three Anatomical Works Attributed to Rufus of Ephesus*, Saarbrücken: LAMBERT Academic Publishing, 2014. Cited here from p. 57 of the doctoral dissertation at the University of Michigan on which this book was based.

3 See Michèle Clément, "De l'anachronisme et du clitoris," *Le Français préclassique*, 13, 2011, pp. 27–45. See also Christian Boudignon, "Vous parlez grec et vous ne le saviez pas," *Connaissance hellénique*, 28, July 7, 2014.

4 Odile Buisson, "Le point G et l'orgasme féminin" [the

G spot and female orgasm], TED talk in Les ERNEST series, June 7, 2014. This remarkable talk questions the existence of the mysterious "G spot."

5 Thomas W. Laqueur, *Making Sex: Body and Gender from the Greeks to Freud*, Cambridge, MA: Harvard University Press, 1990.

6 See Simone de Beauvoir, *The Second Sex*, trans. Constance Borde and Sheila Malovany-Chevallier, New York: Knopf, 2009, II, ch. 4, "The Lesbian." See also Valerie Traub, "The Psychomorphology of the Clitoris": "Since the advent of psychoanalysis, then, the clitoris and the lesbian have been mutually implicated as sisters in shame: each is the disturbing sign (and sign of disturbance) that implies the existence of the other" (*GLQ: A Journal of Lesbian and Gay Studies*, 2, 1995, pp. 81–113, p. 82).

7 For example, Delphine Gardey, *Politique du clitoris*, Paris: Textuel, 2019; Camille Froidevaux-Metterie, *Le corps des femmes: La bataille de l'intime*, Paris: Philosophie Magazine Éditeur, 2018; Maïté Mazaurette and Damien Mascret, *La revanche du clitoris*, Paris: La Musardine, 2016; Clément, "De l'anachronisme et du clitoris"; and Sylvie Chaperon "'Le trône des plaisirs et des voluptés' : anatomie politique du clitoris, de l'Antiquité à la fin du XIXe siècle," *Cahiers d'histoire: Revue d'histoire critique*, 118, 2012, pp. 41–60.

8 Martin Page, *Au-delà de la pénétration*, Paris: Le Nouvel Attila, 2020.

9 Paul B. Preciado, *An Apartment on Uranus: Chronicles of the Crossing*, trans. Charlotte Mandell, South Pasadena, CA: Semiotext(e), 2019, p. 208.

10 As the words suggest, in Jacques Derrida's work, the terms "phallocentrism" and "phallogocentrism" refer to the central role granted to the phallus as symbol. See, for instance, *Glas : Que reste-t-il du savoir absolu?* Paris: Galilée, 1974, pp. 85ff.

11 See Stefanos Milkidis "Foucault: On the Monstrosity of the Hermaphroditic Body," *Queer Cats: Journal of LGBTQ Studies*, 2(1), 2018, pp. 1–12. See also Josée Néron, "Foucault, l'histoire de la sexualité et la condition des femmes dans l'Antiquité," *Les Cahiers de droit*, 36(1), 1995, pp. 246–91.

12 The second volume of Michel Foucault's *The History of Sexuality*, trans. Robert Hurley, New York: Vintage Books, 1990 [1985] addresses *The Use of Pleasure*.

13 For Foucault, the "repressive hypothesis" is the common representation of power as a source of prohibition and censure, particularly of sexuality. Foucault shows how this prohibition in fact creates the very sexuality it represses. See *The History of Sexuality*, I: *An Introduction*, trans. Robert Hurley, New York: Vintage Books, 1990 [1978], p. 15.

14 Gardey, pp. 145–6. Cf. Judith Butler, *Gender Trouble: Feminism and the Subversion of Identity*, New York: Routledge, 1990, pp. 146ff.

15 "Terf" and "swerf" are often associated with each other. Swerf is an acronym for Sex-Worker-Exclusionary Radical Feminist – that is, feminists who denounce prostitution on the grounds that it is a form of oppression.

2 Nymphs 1

1 Adolf Edward Jacobi, *Dictionnaire mythologique universel ou biographie mythique*, trans. Thomas Bernard, Paris: Firmin-Didot, 1854, I, pp. 343–4.
2 Vladimir Nabokov, *Lolita*, New York: Vintage Books, 1997 [1955], p. 16.

3 Nymphs 2

1 Giorgio Agamben, *Nymphs*, trans. Amanda Minervini, London: Seagull Books, 2013.
2 Agamben, p. 49.
3 Agamben, pp. 52–3.
4 Agamben, pp. 40–1.
5 Agamben, p. 43.
6 Agamben, p. 47.
7 Cited in Agamben, p. 51.
8 Agamben, p. 52.
9 Cited in Agamben, p. 51.
10 Agamben, p. 52.
11 Agamben, p. 45.
12 Agamben, p. 46.
13 Agamben, p. 56.
14 Agamben, p. 14.
15 Agamben, pp. 14–15.
16 Agamben, pp. 57–8.

4 Nymphs 3

1 Simone de Beauvoir, *The Second Sex*, trans. Constance Borde and Sheila Malovany-Chevallier, New York: Knopf, 2009, I, p. 193.
2 Beauvoir, I, p. 199.
3 Beauvoir, I, p. 199.
4 André Breton, *Nadja*, Paris: Gallimard, 1964.
5 Breton, p. 130, cited in Beauvoir, I, p. 248.
6 Beauvoir, I, p. 248.
7 Beauvoir, I, p. 248.
8 Beauvoir, I, p. 251.
9 Beauvoir, I, p. 252.
10 Beauvoir, I, p. 252, cited in Breton, p. 375.
11 Beauvoir, I, p. 252.
12 *Archives du surréalisme*, IV: *Recherches sur la sexualité*, ed. José Pierre, NRF-Gallimard, 1991, p. 72.

5 Political Anatomy

1 Pierre-Henri Gouyon, cited in Lise Barnéoud, "Orgasme féminin : on sait d'où il vient," *Science et vie*, 1228, Jan. 2020, p. 106.
2 Gérard Zwang, *Éloge du con : Défense et illustration du sexe féminin*, Paris: La Musardine, 2008, p. 48.
3 "Orgasme féminin : un mystère de l'évolution enfin résolu?" *Science et avenir*, Aug. 3, 2016.
4 Zoe Williams, "The Truth about the Clitoris: Why It's Not Just Built for Pleasure," *Guardian*, Nov. 6, 2019. Cf. also Roy J. Levin, "The Clitoris – An Appraisal of Its Reproductive Function during the Fertile Years: Why

Was It, and Still Is, Overlooked in Accounts of Female Sexual Arousal?" *Clinical Anatomy*, Nov. 5, 2019.

5 Paula Bennett, "Critical Clitoridectomy: Female Sexual Imagery and Feminist Psychoanalytical Theory," *Signs*, 18, 1993, pp. 253–9, p. 257, cited by Valerie Traub in "The Psychomorphology of the Clitoris," *GLQ: A Journal of Lesbian and Gay Studies*, 2, 1995, pp. 81–113, p. 181.

6 A. E. Narjani (Marie Bonaparte), "Considérations sur les causes anatomiques de la frigidité chez la femme" [considerations on the anatomical causes of frigidity in women], *Bruxelles-Médical, Revue bi-hebdomadaire des sciences médicales et chirurgicales*, 27(4), April 1924.

7 Narjani.

6 "Sexual Existence" according to Simone de Beauvoir

1 Jean-Paul Sartre, *Being and Nothingness: A Phenomenological Essay on Ontology*, trans. Hazel E. Barnes, New York: Washington Square Press, 1956, p. 498.

2 Sartre, p. 499.

3 Maurice Merleau-Ponty, *Phenomenology of Perception*, trans. Colin Smith, London: Routledge, 1962, p. 167.

4 Sartre, p. 569.

5 Sartre, p. 516.

6 Sartre, p. 782.

7 Simone de Beauvoir, *The Second Sex*, trans. Constance Borde and Sheila Malovany-Chevallier, New York: Knopf, 2009, II, p. 81.

8 Beauvoir, II, p. 79.
9 Beauvoir, II, p. 283.
10 Beauvoir, II, p. 50.
11 Beauvoir, II, p. 50.
12 Beauvoir, II, p. 68.
13 Beauvoir, II, p. 52.
14 Helene Deutsch, *Psychoanalysis of the Sexual Functions of Women*, trans. Eric Mosbacher, New York: Routledge, 2018 [1991].
15 On this topic, see Marie-Andrée Charbonneau, "La sexualité féminine chez Simone de Beauvoir et Hélène Deutsch," *Simone de Beauvoir Studies*, 21 ("Coast To Coast with Simone de Beauvoir"), Brill, 2004–5, pp. 43–53.
16 Helene Deutsch, *Psychoanalysis of the Sexual Functions of Women*, p. 272.
17 Helene Deutsch, cited in Charbonneau, p. 49.
18 Beauvoir, II, p. 405.
19 Beauvoir, II, p. 405.
20 Beauvoir, II, p. 406.
21 Beauvoir, II, p. 406.

7 Dolto, Lacan and the "Relationship"

1 Françoise Dolto, *Sexualité féminine : la libido génitale et son destin féminin*, Paris: Gallimard, 1996 .
2 "Dialogue préliminaire," in Dolto, *Sexualité féminine*, p. 34.
3 Jacques Lacan and Daniel Lagache, "Guiding Remarks for a Congress on Feminine Sexuality," trans. Bruce Fink, *Écrits: The First Complete Edition in English*,

New York: W.W. Norton & Company Inc., 2006, pp. 610–20.

4 Jacques Lacan, . . . *or Worse: The Seminar of Jacques Lacan Book XIX*, ed. Jacques-Alain Miller, trans. A. R. Price, Cambridge: Polity, 2018, p. 80.

5 Lacan, . . . *or Worse*, p. 80.

6 Jacques Lacan, *Le séminaire, livre XVII : L'envers de la psychanalyse 1969–1970*, ed. Jacques-Alain Miller, Paris: Seuil, 1991, p. 134.

7 Translator's note: I am using the translation of the phrase recently employed as a title by Alain Badiou and Barbara Cassin, *There is No Such Thing as a Sexual Relationship: Two Lessons on Lacan*, New York: Columbia University Press, 2017.

8 Lacan, *Le séminaire*, p. 21.

9 Lacan, *Le séminaire*, p. 21.

10 Jacques Lacan, "Le séminaire XXIV : L'insu que sait de l'une-bévue s'aile à mourre," 1976–7, unpublished, available online, p. 6.

11 Lacan, . . . *or Worse,* p. 80.

12 Jacques Lacan, *The Object Relation: The Seminar of Jacques Lacan, Book IV*, trans. Adrian R. Price, Cambridge, UK, and Medford, MA: Polity, 2020, p. 41.

13 Lacan, "Guiding Remarks," pp. 612–13.

14 Dolto, *Sexualité féminine*, p. 91.

15 Dolto, *Sexualité féminine*, p. 83.

16 Dolto, *Sexualité féminine*, p. 88.

17 Dolto, *Sexualité féminine*, p. 88.

18 Dolto, *Sexualité féminine*, p. 90.

19 Dolto, *Sexualité féminine*, p. 172.

20 The remarks are recounted by Magali Taïeb-Cohen in "Ce que les femmes doivent à Dolto," Colloque de la Fondation Européenne pour la Psychanalyse, online text, p. 7.

21 Caroline Eliacheff, *Françoise Dolto : Une journée particulière*, Paris: Flammarion, 2018, p. 181.

22 "Entretien avec Jean-Pierre Winter," cited in Eliacheff, *Françoise Dolto : Une journée particulière*, pp. 183–4.

8 "The Feminine Sexual Organ Is the Clitoris"

1 The quotation in the chapter title above is from Carla Lonzi, the opening words of *La donna clitoridea e la donna vaginale e altri scritti*, published in 1971 and then in *Sputiamo su Hegel! La donna clitoridea e la donna vaginale e altri scritti*, Milan: Scritti di Rivolta Femminile, 1974, pp. 74–170; republished Milan: Et al. Edizioni, 2010, p. 3 (the translations of *La donna clitoridea* in this chapter are mine, but from Catherine Malabou's French translations, since this work does not exist in French).

2 Cited in Michèle Causse and Maryvonne Lapouge (eds.), *Écrits, voix d'Italie*, Paris: Des Femmes, 1977.

3 Carla Lonzi, *Let's Spit on Hegel!* trans. Veronica Newman, Milan: Rivolta Femminile, 1970, https://my-blackout.com/2020/11/18/carla-lonzi-lets-spit-on-hegel.

4 Lonzi, *Let's Spit on Hegel!*

5 Lonzi, *La donna clitoridea* (Translator's note: following existing translations, I use the neologism "clitoridian," rather than the standard medical "clitoral" in discus-

sions of Lonzi's work, to signal a political commitment to feminism).

6 Lonzi, *La donna clitoridea*, p. 12.
7 Lonzi, *La donna clitoridea*, p. 2.
8 Lonzi, *La donna clitoridea*, p. 13.
9 Lonzi, *La donna clitoridea*, p. 12.
10 Lonzi, *La donna clitoridea*, p. 12.
11 Lonzi, *La donna clitoridea*, p. 13.
12 Lonzi, *La donna clitoridea*, p. 12.
13 Cited in Claire Fontaine, "We Are All Clitoridian Women: Notes on Carla Lonzi's Legacy," e-flux journal, 47, September 2013, online edition, p. 6. The quote is taken from Lonzi's diary, *Taci, anzi parla: Diario di una feminista* [shut up, no speak: a feminist's diary], Milan: Scritti di Rivolta Femminile, 1978, p. 9.
14 Lonzi, *La donna clitoridea*, p. 14.
15 Lonzi, *La donna clitoridea*, p. 21.
16 Lonzi, *La donna clitoridea*, p. 7.
17 Lonzi, *La donna clitoridea*, p. 4.
18 Lonzi, *La donna clitoridea*, p. 6.
19 Lonzi, *La donna clitoridea*, p. 8.
20 Lonzi, *Taci, anzi parla*, p. 267. Quoted and translated by Elena Dalla Torre, in "The clitoris diaries: *la donna clitoridea,* feminine authenticity, and the phallic allegory of Carla Lonzi's radical feminism," *European Journal of Women's Studies*, 21(3), 2014, pp. 219–32, p. 227.

9 Luce Irigaray

1   Luce Irigaray, *Speculum of the Other Woman*, trans. Gillian C. Gill, Ithaca, NY: Cornell University Press, 1985, p. 229.

2   Luce Irigaray, *This Sex which Is Not One*, trans. Catherine Porter with Carolyn Burke, Ithaca, NY: Cornell University Press, 1985, p. 28.

3   Irigaray, *This Sex which Is Not One*, p. 28.

4   Irigaray, *This Sex which Is Not One*, p. 26.

5   Luce Irigaray, *An Ethics of Sexual Difference*, trans. Carolyn Burke and Gillian C. Gill, Ithaca, NY: Cornell University Press, 1993, p. 119.

6   Irigaray, *Ethics*, p. 5.

7   Irigaray, *Speculum*, p. 296.

8   Irigaray, *Speculum*, p. 230.

9   Irigaray, *Speculum*, p. 233.

10 Irigaray, *This Sex which Is Not One*, p. 28.

11 Irigaray, *This Sex which Is Not One*, p. 23.

12 Irigaray, *This Sex which Is Not One*, p. 26.

13 Irigaray, *Speculum*, p. 233.

14 Valerie Traub, "The Psychomorphology of the Clitoris," *GLQ: A Journal of Lesbian and Gay Studies*, 2, 1995, pp. 81–113, p. 102.

15 Traub, p. 102.

16 Irigaray, *Speculum*, p. 231.

17 Irigaray, *This Sex which Is Not One*, p. 71.

18 Irigaray, *This Sex which Is Not One*, p. 207.

19 Audre Lorde, "An Interview with Audre Lorde," *American Poetry Review*, 9(2), 1980, p. 21.

10 "With Tenderness and Respect for the Blameless Vulva"

1 The quotation in the chapter title comes from Alice Walker. She opens her novel *Possessing the Secret of Joy*, New York: Harcourt Brace Jovanovich, 1992, with the dedication, "with tenderness and respect for the blameless vulva."

   For the 2018 Report: Maryvonne Blondin and Marta de Cidrac, "Rapport d'information fait au nom de la délégation aux droits des femmes et à l'égalité des chances entre les hommes et les femmes sur les mutilations sexuelles féminines" [report on female sexual mutilations, prepared by the delegation for the rights of women and equal opportunity], *Sénat*, 479, Ordinary Session 2017–18, recorded at the Senate Presidency on May 16, 2018, accessible online.

2 Blondin and Cidrac, "Rapport," p. 9.

3 Blondin and Cidrac, "Rapport," pp. 9–10. A United Nations seminar held in Burkina Faso in 1991 on "Pratiques affectant la santé des femmes et des enfants" [practices affecting the health of women and children] recommended the permanent adoption of the term FGM as a replacement for the expression "female circumcision."

4 Blondin and Cidrac, "Rapport," p. 12.

5 Blondin and Cidrac, "Rapport," p. 20.

6 Blondin and Cidrac, "Rapport," p. 138.

7 Halimata Fofana, *Mariama, l'écorchée vive*, Paris, Karthala, 2015. Cited in Blondin and Cidrac, "Rapport," p. 5.

8 Alice Walker, *Possessing the Secret of Joy*, New York: Harcourt, Brace Jovanovich Publishers, 1992.

9 Alice Walker and Pratibha Parmar, *Warrior Marks: Female Genital Mutilation and the Sexual Blinding of Women*. New York: Harcourt, Brace, 1993. The documentary by the same name is available on Vimeo.

10 Quoted by Tobe Levin in "Alice Walker, Activist: Matron of FORWARD," in Maria Diedrich, Henri Louis Gates and Carl Pedersen (eds.), *Black Imagination and the Middle Passage*, W. E. B. Dubois Institute series, New York and Oxford: Oxford University Press, 1999, pp. 240–54, p. 240.

11 Elfriede Jelinek, *Waging Empathy: Alice Walker, Possessing the Secret of Joy, and the Global Movement to Ban FGM*, trans. Tobe Levin, Frankfurt am Main: UnCUT/VOICES Press, 2014, p. 5.

12 Walker, *Possessing the Secret of Joy*, p. 3.

13 Walker, *Possessing the Secret of Joy*, pp. 108–9.

14 Walker, *Possessing the Secret of Joy*, p. 73.

15 Audre Lorde, "Your Silence Will Not Protect You," in *Sister Outsider*, New York: Trumansburg, Crossing Press, 1984, p. 41.

16 Toni Morrison, *Beloved,* NY: Knopf, 1987.

17 Walker, *Possessing the Secret of Joy*, p. 106.

18 bell hooks, *Sisters of the Yam: Black Women and Self-Recovery*, New York: Routledge, 2015, pp. 121–2.

19 hooks, *Sisters of the Yam*, p. 125.

11 Mutilation and Repair

1 See, for example, "The hearing by Docteur Ghada Hatem, founder of *La Maison des femmes de Saint-Denis*, on December 14, 2017, showed that it is very difficult to separate the issue of sexual mutilation from violence against women in general and that excision lies on the continuum of these forms of violence, with forced marriage, rape, especially conjugal rape, and violence within the family": Blondin and Cidrac, "Rapport," p. 1.

2 In English, "Disorders of Sex Development" (DSD). The French equivalent is *Troubles du Développement sexuel* (TDS) (difficulties in sexual development) or *Troubles de la Différence Sexuelle* (sexual difference difficulties). A preferable term is *variations du développement sexuel* (variations in sexual development) since it avoids all negative connotation. The term "disorders" or "variations" is used when an individual's biological sexual characteristics (chromosomic, hormonal, anatomical) differ from established gender norms.

3 Brian D. Earp and Sara Johnsdotter, "Current Critiques of the WHO Policy on Female Genital Mutilation," *International Journal of Impotence Research*, 2021, pp. 196–209.

4 Earp and Johnsdotter, p. 197.

5 Earp and Johnsdotter, p. 197.

6 Earp and Johnsdotter, p. 197.

7 Earp and Johnsdotter, p. 197.

8 Earp and Johnsdotter, pp. 197–8.

9 "Male genital cutting (MGC) ranges from ritual prick-

ing (e.g., *hatafat dam brit*), to piercing, scraping the inside of the urethra, bloodletting, shaft scarring, and/or foreskin slitting (among, e.g., various ethnic groups in Papua New Guinea) . . . to forced circumcision of men following political conflict in various countries, to subincision . . . in Aboriginal Australia, to castration (now rare but still occasionally documented among the *hijras* of India), and amputations": Earp and Johnsdotter, p. 198.

10 To say nothing of the term "repair, used to describe reconstructive procedures for genitalia. What exactly is a "repaired woman"?

11 Delphine Gardey, *Politique du clitoris*, Paris: Textuel, 2019, p. 90.

12 Technologically Modified Bodies

1 Paul B. Preciado, *Countersexual Manifesto*, trans. Kevin Gerry Dunn, New York: Columbia University Press, 2018 [2000].

2 Paul B. Preciado, *Testo Junkie: Sex, Drugs and Biopolitics in the Pharmapornographic Era*, trans. Bruce Benderson, New York: The Feminist Press, 2013 [2008].

3 Preciado, *An Apartment on Uranus*.

4 Paul B. Preciado, *Can the Monster Speak? Report to an Academy of Psychoanalysts*, trans. Frank Wynne, South Pasadena, CA: Semiotext(e), 2021.

5 Paul B. Preciado, "Trans-fem.i.nism," *Purple Magazine*, F/W24, 2015, p. 1.

6 The term was the invention of the doctor and soci-

ologist Volkmar Sigusch, who used it in his articles "Die Transsexuellen und unser nosomorpher Blick I," *ZfS*, 4(3), 1991, pp. 225–56, and "The Neosexual Revolution," in *Archives of Social Behavior*, 27, 1998, pp. 331–59.

7 To be precise, these adjectives refer to the location of Gaul from the perspective of Rome. Ultimately, the meaning of the locations of "transalpine" and "cisalpine" depends on one's perspective.

8 Preciado, "Trans-fem.i.nism," p. 1.

9 Preciado, "Trans-fem.i.nism," p. 4. Cf., on this point, also Gayle Salamon, *Assuming a Body: Transgender and Rhetorics of Materiality*, New York: Columbia University Press, 2010.

10 Judith Butler, *Bodies that Matter: On the Discursive Limits of Sex*, New York: Routledge, 2011.

11 Preciado, *Countersexual Manifesto*, p. 28.

12 Preciado, *Countersexual Manifesto*, p. 21.

13 Preciado, *Countersexual Manifesto*, p. 24.

14 Preciado, *Can the Monster Speak?* p. 34.

15 Preciado, *Can the Monster Speak?* p. 11.

16 Preciado, *Can the Monster Speak?* pp. 63–4.

13 Nymphs 4

1 Lars von Trier, *Nymphomaniac*, I and II, 2013.

14 Ecstasy Zones in the Real

1 Catherine Malabou, *Changing Difference: The Feminine and the Question of Philosophy*, trans. Carolyn Shread, Cambridge, UK: Polity, 2011.

2 "Feminine thought tends to adopt the position of a neutral *logos*. From the moment that it was a matter of demonstrating truth and justice, the idea that being male or female made no difference emerged primarily in the feminine mind; it is not therefore simply by chance that it is more often expressed by women than by men": Luisa Muraro, "Le penseur neutre était une femme" [the neutral thinker was a woman], *Langages*, 85, 1987, pp. 35–40, p. 35.

3 Jacques Rancière, *Dis-Agreement: Politics and Philosophy*, trans. Julie Rose, Minneapolis: University of Minnesota Press, 1999, p. 36.

4 Rancière, *Dis-Agreement*, p. 36.

5 Silvia Federici, *Caliban and the Witch: Women, the Body and Primitive Accumulation*, Brooklyn, NY: Autonomedia, 2004.

6 Silvia Federici, *Beyond the Periphery of the Skin: Rethinking, Remaking, and Reclaiming the Body in Contemporary Capitalism*, Oakland, CA: PM Press, 2020.

7 Federici, *Beyond the Periphery of the Skin*, p. 2.

8 Mara Mantanaro, "Corps résistants et puissants chez Silvia Federici: une stratégie d'insurrection féministe. À propos de *Par-delà les frontières du corps: Repenser, refaire et revendiquer le corps dans le capitalisme tardif*, de Silvia Federici," *Contretemps: Revue de critique com-*

muniste, June 18, 2020. Cf. also Elsa Dorlin, "Vers une épistémologie des résistances," in Elsa Dorlin, ed., *Sexe, race, classe : Pour une épistémologie de la domination*, Paris: Presses universitaires de France, 2009.

9 Mantanaro, "Corps résistants," p. 4.

10 Preciado, *Can the Monster Speak?* p. 26.

11 Preciado, *Can the Monster Speak?* pp. 40–1.

12 Judith/Jack Halberstam, "Transgender Butch: Butch/FTM Border Wars and the Masculine Continuum," *GLQ: A Journal of Lesbian and Gay Studies*, 4(2), 1998, pp. 287–310, p. 287.

13 Halberstam, "Transgender Butch," p. 289.

14 Halberstam, "Transgender Butch," p. 289.

15 In "Transgender Butch," Halberstam concludes as follows: "there are a variety of gender-outlaw bodies under the sign of non-normative masculinities and femininities. The task at hand is not to decide which of these represents the place of most resistance but to begin the work of documenting their distinctive feature," pp. 291–2.

16 Jacques Derrida, *Mémoires : For Paul de Man*, trans. Cecile Lindsay, Jonathan Culler and Eduardo Cadava, New York: Columbia University Press, 1986, pp. 72ff.

17 *Point[s] d'accroche*, online journal: "Comment devenir et s'affirmer sujet entre le pénis puissant et le clitoris érectile," editorial posted by Céline Guilleux on April 29, 2015.

18 Another question from the conveners: "Is the stereotype of the 'powerful' woman promoted by the political, economic and cultural world truly an example of liberation? Isn't it just the opposite of the stereotype of the

dominated woman, in the same way that mother and whore are two sides of the same coin, both serving to distance a threatening feminine?" They also recall that "in 2008, in the issue of *Cahiers du genre* dedicated to '*Les fleurs du mâle. Masculinités sans hommes*?' [flowers of male/violence. Masculinities without men]," Marie Hélène / Sam Bourcier and Pascale Molinier asked the following question: "Is masculinity the future of woman?" By "masculinity," they are referring to a "source of *empowerment* and pleasure," claiming that "when invested positively, it is one of the possible forms of transformation of class, gender, race and sex identities for individuals assigned as women."

19 Preciado, *An Apartment on Uranus*, pp. 213–14.
20 Roland Barthes, *Camera Lucida: Reflections on Photography*, trans. Richard Howard, New York: Hill and Wang, 2010, pp. 27–8.
21 Barthes, *Camera Lucida*, p. 27.
22 Barthes, *Camera Lucida*, pp. 26–7.
23 Barthes, *Camera Lucida*, p. 26.

15 Clitoris, Anarchy and the Feminine

1 Pierre Joseph Proudhon, *Les confessions d'un révolutionnaire, pour servir à l'histoire de la révolution de février*, Paris: Hachette livre BNF, 2012.

Index

143